Robert T

SYDNEY

DISCOVER THE CITY

Photographs by Lukas Roth and Ben Apfelbaum

Major Mitchell Press

ISBN 0 9587708 1 6

Contents

*Chapter numbers correspond to numbers on map

Introduction

Sydney is intended to help you understand the city — to appreciate the historic and modern buildings, as well as its famous Opera House and Harbour Bridge, the outdoor life found on its vast beaches, golf courses, wildlife sanctuaries and national parks.

The city's climate is mild and sub-tropical. It is located on the south-east coast of the continent of Australia, latitude 34 degrees east, longitude 151 degrees south. Summers start in October, last 6 months, and are hot and enjoyable. Winters are mild, usually sunny, start in June and last around two months. Springs and Autumns are beautiful and brief, but may be rainy.

There are over 3.5 million people living in Greater Sydney — bounded by the Blue Mountains to the west, the Pacific Ocean to the east and the jade-green forests of the National Parks to the north and south. Six hundred suburbs sprawl in-between, where its citizens are accommodated in 1 million dwellings — suburban houses, blocks of home units (apartments), and rows of older 'terrace' houses closer to the city.

While the city has grown from an English-speaking settlement founded 200 years ago, nearly 30 per cent of today's inhabitants were born outside Australia and have arrived since World War Two — mainly from Britain, Ireland, Italy, Greece, Spain, Poland, Yugoslavia, Holland, Germany, China, Latin America, Lebanon and South-East Asia. This multi-racial mix makes for an exotic cosmopolitan metropolis, with each culture contributing something to Sydney life.

1   The Sydney Opera House

Contrary to its name, the Opera House is not a 'building', but a *group* of buildings spread over an area of 4.5 hectares (11¼ acres). It contains five theatre halls, a reception hall and exhibition hall, five rehearsal studios, three restaurants, six theatre bars, a number of foyers, and loungerooms, 60 dressing rooms, a library, administration offices, plant and machinery areas, store-rooms, bathrooms, kitchens, canteens, complete suites, an art gallery and a souvenir shop.

'I had white in mind when I designed the Opera House,' — the building's creator, Danish architect Jörn Utzon once explained, — 'And I saw the roof, like sails, white in the strong day, the whole thing slowly coming to life as the sun shone from the east and lifted overhead. In the hot sun of the day it will be a beautiful, white shimmering thing — as alive to the eyes as architecture can make anything, set in the blue-green waters of the harbour. And at night the floodlit shells will be equally vibrant — but in a softer, more majestic way.'

Following a 1957 competition for a performing arts building on the site of Bennelong Point *(see Harbour Islands story)*, Jörn Utzon's design was accepted before anyone realised just how revolutionary his concept was. Inspired by the architecture of the East and of Aztec Mexico, Utzon had submitted the dramatic

The Opera House seen from the western side of the Harbour

outlines of some elliptical roofs on a rectangular base surrounded by the waters of Sydney Harbour. After 16 years of planning, and 14 years of construction paid for by public lotteries, the Sydney Opera House was inaugurated with great pomp by Queen Elizabeth II in 1973.

The complex is comprised of four units.

The Western Shells. A set of four 'sails' on the Harbour Bridge side, placed on top of the podium, covering the roof and walls of the Concert Hall beneath it.

Each shell of the complex is made up of concrete sections, every one of which, poured on site, is like a segment of orange skin. The 2,194 sections are held together by 350 kilometres (210 miles) of cables, and collectively weigh 26,800 tonnes. The tip of the tallest shell reaches 66 metres (214 feet) above sea level — almost 9 metres (29 feet) higher than the centre of the Harbour Bridge's roadway.

Over 1 million tiles cover the shells of the complex

The Eastern Shells. A set of four shells erected on the side of the Royal Botanic Gardens, sheltering the ceiling and walls of the Opera Theatre inside it.

Each shell is covered with hundreds of thousands of cream-coloured tiles, of varying sizes. The glossy reflective surface waterproofs the building and gives it the shimmer the pyramids of Egypt and Mexico once had before their own tiles were lost numerous centuries ago. In all 1,056,000 Swedish-made tiles, designed according architect Utzon's specifications, were used.

The Southern Shells. A set of two smaller shells houses the main restaurant, giving its capacity of 250 diners a classic harbour view through the building's glass walls.

The podium. The base which rises above the water and supports the shells is 186 metres (604½ feet) long, 116 metres (377 feet) wide and 20 metres (65 feet) high. Its outside is covered with about 10,000 slabs of reconstituted pink granite. It is supported by 550 concrete piers and 32 columns, many of them sunk to more than 21 metres below sea-level.

Inside, the podium is multi-levelled, with about 3 hectares (7½ acres) of usable floor space, and contains nearly 1,000 rooms connected by a honeycomb of doorways, stairwells, corridors, tunnels, steps, ladders, lift shafts, passageways, overpasses, curved corridors, inclines and overhanging platforms.

The Opera Theatre seats 1,547, is painted black and contains the world's largest theatre curtain: 16 metres (52 feet) long and 8 metres (26 feet) wide — featuring a sun motif, the work of

View of Sydney Harbour from the northern foyer

artist John Coburn. On its stage have appeared some of the world's finest singers in works by Mozart, Verdi, Wagner, Puccini and dozens of other composers.

The corridors display portraits of famous performers, while the northern foyer of the theatre features a giant Aboriginal mural by Michael Tjakamarra, entitled 'Possum Dreaming'. The work, in earth and sky colours, 10 metres (33 feet) by 1.8 metres (6 feet), depicts the secret ceremonial rites of the Western Desert tribes.

The Concert Hall seats 2,690 and is lined with timber, with a ceiling rising 25 metres (81 feet) above the stage. The Hall also contains a grand organ with five manuals and pedal, with approximately 10,500 pipes, 109 of which are visible from the auditorium.

Its northern foyer displays a mural entitled 'Five Bells' by the artist John Olsen. Depicting disparate elements of Sydney Harbour such as night lights, rocks, fish, children on the beach, aboriginal art, the work has at its core a famous Australian poem.

As a complex dedicated to the performing arts, to congresses, exhibitions and to eating, the Opera House can contain about 7,000 spectators, performers, staff and restaurant diners at any one time. Each of its auditoriums is acoustically insulated, so that four different performances may occur simultaneously — while outside ferries, international container ships and ocean liners ply the waters of the Harbour, and thousands of visitors throng the harbourside souvenir shops, cafes and promenades.

'Possum Dreaming' by Tjakamarra in the Opera's foyer

2 Government House, home of the State Governor

Erected in 1838 for the Governors of New South Wales on a high ridge at the western side of the Botanic Gardens, this building's best-known features are its turrets and 'medieval' castellated edges, thick stone walls, diamond lead-lighted windows, and forbidding martial air.

In its prominent situation, the British-designed Government House was for years the distinctive landmark at the approach to Sydney Cove. Most of the sandstone used was quarried at Pyrmont, while the cedar came from the Hunter and Shoalhaven areas of the State.

The interior ground-plan is still largely original, with an impressive red cedar staircase, and 33-metre-long (107 feet) reception room. The eastern facade is graced with a cloister and the stone carved coats-of-arms of former Governors. The beautifully laid out gardens have an extensive view of the Harbour.

The most exciting moment in the building's history came in 1912, when the State government locked out all vice-regal representatives, incorporated the building's grounds into the Botanic Gardens, and threw open Government House to the public as a museum. After conflict and litigation the building was returned to its role as the residence of the State's Governor.

Home of the Queen's representative in New South Wales

The Conservatorium of Music

Like an antic fortress, this building rises at the top of Bridge Street on the edge of the Botanic Gardens. The doors are usually open, and music lovers, visitors and students from other countries are welcome to attend concerts and recitals.

The structure of this intriguing building was designed by Francis Greenway about the time that Napoleon lost the battle of Waterloo (1816). Wanting to please the Colony's Scottish master, Governor Lachlan Macquarie, Greenway — who had been exiled to Australia for forgery — modelled the building on *Inverary Castle*. The construction was done, of course, by the convicts. Macquarie, an autocrat, spent a large sum of official money on the building — even though most of Sydney at the time lived in indescribable poverty and misery. Then, to add insult to injury, on the building's completion he announced that the 'fortress' — far from housing himself and his family — was merely intended for his stable of 30 horses and the numerous people attending them. The elaborate edifice continued as the Governor's stables for almost a century when, in 1913, in a wave of republican feeling, the N.S.W. Government nationalised it, turning it over to the State's youth for their continued use and enjoyment.

A colonial legacy: the Music Conservatorium

4 Monument to Governor Phillip

On the west side of the Royal Botanic Gardens off Macquarie Street, stands the statue of Governor Arthur Phillip, (1738-1814), in a larger-than-life size bronze made some 75 years after his death by the Italian sculptor Achille Simonetti and cast in Florence, Italy, by the master F. Galli.

Phillip (the founder of white civilisation in Australia) gazes from his high pedestal, (Royal parchment in hand and flag under arm), across the land where he began the first soil cultivation in Sydney, and beyond that to the harbour, which he was the first sea captain to enter at the head of his fleet.

On the 26 January 1788, once all the eleven ships of that First Fleet were safely anchored in Sydney Cove (Circular Quay), the disembarkation of groups of convicts began. Confusion and excitement reigned everywhere. Ten days later the settlement was ready for the women and children to come ashore. The Governor's prefabricated residence was also erected.

When all 1,360 persons had been landed, Phillip ordered the whole colony to assemble for the reading of a Royal letter which appointed him as Governor in Chief over the territory called New South Wales, at the time comprising about 3,500,000 square kilometres (2,100,000 square miles), or half of Australia.

The newly proclaimed Governor then addressed the assembly, telling them he would treat well those who worked hard, and would show no mercy to those who committed new crimes. He urged the men and women of the Colony to marry, and to conform to Christian principles and beliefs.

The advice was partly taken and in the following week fourteen marriages were recorded, while Captain Phillip went to explore the harbour and rivers around Sydney Cove in order to extend the colony.

Ever since, 26 January has been celebrated as *Anniversary Day* — becoming known over the years as *Australia Day*. On this date the whole continent ceases work, festivities are held, and at certain times the landing at Sydney Cove is re-enacted in eighteenth century costume.

When Phillip departed Sydney five years later, the population had increased to 3,120 — of whom 2,465 were convicts. The small town of Sydney was securely established. It had survived because of Phillip's strong and sober personality, and this is how the monument by Simonetti portrays him.

The fountain at his feet, also the work of Simonetti, is in the Victorian Baroque style, and was unveiled during Queen Victoria's Jubilee celebrations, when the British Empire still looked invincible and everlasting. The elaborate collection of nautical motifs and classical deities around the fountain echo such values. Bronze reliefs represent Justice, Patriotism and Education, the three slogans under which Britain sent out her children to conquer the world.

Flanking these are four figures symbolic of some of the means by which Sydney's citizens enriched themselves: Neptune (shipping), Agriculture (cereals and timber), the one-eyed Cyclops (sheep farming), and Commerce (gold and metals). These are accompanied by dolphins, and four bronze plaques of Aboriginals.

Governor Phillip announcing foundation of new colony

The Royal Botanic Gardens

The major preoccupation for the members of the First Fleet arriving in 1788 was survival. In these first years most soldiers and their charges were in a state of continual starvation. It was simply not known how to make European vegetables and plants grow in the new climate. The large farming area set aside on the hill overlooking the harbour was worked and re-worked until, step-by-step, some progress was made. Within a few years the farms were moved inland to Parramatta, and in 1816 the hill beside the city — scene of intense suffering — was established as a garden, the basis of today's Royal Botanic Gardens.

The Gardens (open every day to the public from morning until sunset) today rank among the world's oldest and most important. Thousands of Australian plants and flowers are on exhibition, along with imported plants, herbs and trees. They are not only a scenic attraction and an opportunity for visitors to inspect the continent's flora, but also play a significant role in scientific research — particularly of species threatened by human activity.

The Gardens encompass an area of 30 hectares (74 acres) and are flanked on their southern, western and eastern sides by the 34 hectares (84 acres) of the Domain — one of Sydney's public parks. Entry to the Gardens can be made from the Opera House, the harbour shores, Mrs Macquarie's Road, the Art Gallery of New South Wales, Shakespeare Place and Macquarie Street.

A pathway among the world's greatest collection of palms

The Gardens are divided into three sections. The Upper Garden, to the south, is mainly for scientific research, and contains the 1899 Herbarium with its original specimens — some collected by the 1770 botanists Joseph Banks and Daniel Solander.

The Middle Garden follows the shape of the original farms established here in 1788. It contains palms, spring flowers, a kiosk, a stream, and a small memorial pond.

The Lower Garden, with more ponds, flower-beds and extensive lawns, reaches down to the Harbour. Here nature and the city vista evoke a splendid range of moods.

Walking the paths the visitor encounters many birds — among them the White Ibis, Black Duck, Rainbow Lorikeet, Yellow-Crested Cockatoo, Laughing Kookaburra and brightly tinted Rosella. The Rose Garden and hothouses are other features.

The Gardens possess the greatest variety of palms — many imported — growing together anywhere in the world. Palms are botanical flags in the Sydney scenery — reminders that the city is on the shores of the South Pacific, and is a sub-tropical city. The two best-known Sydney species are the Bangalow Palm (*Archontophoenix cunninghamiana*) with feather-shaped fronds, and the Cabbage Tree Palm (*Livistona australis*) — with leaves shaped like a fan, and used by convicts to build houses and make hats.

Australian rainforest (jungle) species such as the enormous Moreton Bay Figs (*Ficus macrophylla*) and the Port Jackson Figs

Visitors Centre in the Botanic Gardens

Orchids, ferns and palms in an exotic setting

Right: The Gardens' Palace Gates on Macquarie Street. The gates are all that is left of a grand international exhibition building which burnt down in the nineteenth century

Shaded groves flourish throughout the seasons

(*Ficus rubiginosa*) — the largest of which grows on Lawn 44 — can also be found. On Lawn 29 stands the remarkable Queensland Bottle Tree (*Brachychiton rupestris*), with its bizarre swollen trunk. Perhaps the most famous of all Australian rainforest trees, the Red Cedar (*Toona australis*) — used for so much of the early building and furniture-construction in Australia — is found on Lawn 24.

Mrs Macquarie's Chair

The 200-metre (650 feet) wide promontory at the end of the Royal Botanic Gardens on the western side of Woolloomooloo Bay is a headland with panoramic views, named Mrs Macquarie's Point.

Mrs Macquarie was the wife of one of the colonial Governors. Thinking she was coming to Sydney for only 3 or 4 years, she in fact remained for 12; and during this time helped her husband transform the place from a penal settlement into a town. An accomplished woman, she was responsible for the look and style of buildings such as the Old Mint and the State Parliament House.

In 1816 the Governor had a carriage road built to the point so that his wife could better enjoy the magnificent harbour views. Near the lookout, a seat was carved from the rock and named Mrs Macquarie's Chair.

All Sydney children have at some point in their lives been taken to this spot. To sit on the Chair is one of the city's real traditions — along with a meat pie snack from the little take-away food stand called Harry's Cafe de Wheels in nearby Woolloomooloo, and a visit to the boomerang throwers and snake men out at La Perouse on Botany Bay.

Mrs Macquarie's Chair: grand vistas of the Harbour

7 Henry Lawson in the Domain

The Sydney Domain is a large public park east and south of the Royal Botanic Gardens. It is a traditional meeting place for protests, rallies, political demonstrations and Sunday-afternoon oratory in the style of London's Hyde Park Corner.

In 1856 a French balloonist was lynched here because his balloon would not rise; in 1917 (during World War One) the entire town gathered to protest army conscription. In 1931 over 100,000 people massed to oppose the State Governor; and in 1975 there was again mass crowding to protest the Governor General.

Along Art Gallery Road, near the eastern entrance of the Botanic Gardens, stands the monument to the half-Norwegian journalist Henry Lawson ('Larsen'). Born to immigrant parents when Australia was still a collection of colonies, in 1867, Lawson died in Sydney 55 years later, when the country had become an independent nation. During his hard life he wrote hundreds of works on the feelings of the homeless, the unemployed and the exploited factory and land workers.

Sculpted by George Lambert, the statue was erected to Lawson's memory in 1930. It depicts the writer in the company of a bushman and his dog

The Art Gallery of New South Wales

This extensive complex is situated on Art Gallery Road, in exotic and tropical scenery on the edge of the Domain. Architect Horbury Hunt began the building in 1885, and additions were made some years later by Walter Vernon, the building acquiring its present facade of Pyrmont sandstone columns during the first decade of the twentieth century. The Gallery was extended again 60 years later by Andrew Andersons, and is now large enough to house extensive collections of both Australian and international works.

Ornamenting the sides of the building are the names of painters, sculptors and architects who exerted their influence on the world of 1900. An incomplete series of bronze reliefs depict various periods in the art history of Assyria, Egypt, Greece and Rome. Equestrian statues on the sides of the entrance symbolise peace and war. Palm trees, lush vegetation and the waters of the Harbour form the building's greater, general setting.

Entrance to the Gallery with 'Offerings of Peace' by Bayes

'A Summer's Morning' by Rupert Bunny (1864-1946). Oil on canvas (c. 1908). Bunny was born in Melbourne but spent most of his working life abroad, mainly in France. His paintings echo the sentiments of the Pre-Raphaelites in their refined graceful figures

English Art. These works, in the Old Courts, are the initial canvases which formed the Gallery's first cluster of paintings. The most famous piece here is the 1876 *Chaucer at the Court of Edward III* by Ford Madox Brown, a painting which was influential in the creation of the Pre-Raphaelite movement. There are also works by Lord Leighton, G. F. Watts, Edward Poynter and representatives of the Royal Academy.

Old Masters. Included here are portraits by William Hogarth and Joshua Reynolds; Renaissance sculptures by Francesco di Simone Ferrucci and Sano di Pietro; and, notably *The Release of St Peter* by Bernardo Strozzi, painted in Venice around 1635 and charged with all the elements of Baroque realism.

Australian Art (in the Old Courts). First hall includes paintings by John Webber, a companion of the navigator James Cook; Conrad Martens, Sydney's first painter; W. C. Piguenit, John Glover and J.S. Prout, all of whom depicted Australia faithfully — but in a gentle European light and with idealised landscapes.

Second hall: forms a collection of the first genuinely *Australian* steps in modern art, housed in the elegant and bright hall created in 1902 by the architect W. L. Vernon; paintings by Tom Roberts and Arthur Streeton, two of the country's best loved artists — *The Golden Fleece* by Roberts, about life in a sheep shearing shed, is one of Australia's most famous paintings; Frederick McCubbin's *On the Wallaby Track*, a melancholy work about the struggling pioneers, is the most frequently-visited painting in the Gallery. Other prominent paintings in this court are E. Phillips Fox's beautiful *The Ferry*, Rupert Bunny's *A Summer Morning* and *Summer time*, and Hugh Ramsay's provocative *The Sisters*.

'Holiday Sketch at Coogee' by Tom Roberts (1856-1931). Oil on canvas (c. 1888). Born in England he was the most prominent member of the famous Heidelberg School

'Sydney Harbour' by John D. Moore. Oil on canvas (c. 1936)

'Nude Washing in a Creek III' (1961) by Arthur Boyd (1920- ?)

The Tribal Galleries. This is a collection of tribal art from Melanesia, Papua New Guinea and Aboriginal Australia. On show are ceremonial objects, totemic poles and bark paintings — presented in a suitably darkened and sympathetic atmosphere.

European Twentieth Century Art. This comprises a series of paintings tracing the developments of modern European art from the turn of the century to the death of Picasso. Canvases by Pissaro, Braque, Vlaminck, Kandinsky, Leger, Dufy, Bonnard and Picasso.

Australian Twentieth Century Art. Works by significant Australian painters, created mainly during the past 50 years. The best-known painter of the period, Sidney Nolan, is represented with several canvases. His series on the nineteenth century terrorist Ned Kelly has earned him worldwide fame. Equally well-known in Australia are William Dobell, a painter with a fine satirical flair; Russell Drysdale, who captured the sense of isolation of the Australian individual; and Donald Friend, who brought the public closer to the art of South-East Asia.

'The Camp' by Sidney Nolan (1917- ?). Oil on canvas (1978). The police sets up camp in pursuit of the masked Ned Kelly, who is invisible to their eyes. Born in Melbourne, Nolan received great critical acclaim around the world for his Kelly series

9 Monument to Shakespeare

The study and enjoyment of the works of the English poet and dramatist William Shakespeare is sacrosanct to the Australian education. No child can escape him — no school examination is complete without a detailed study of one of his poems or plays. Australia may be independent of Great Britain — but it is not independent of William Shakespeare. What Marx is to the Communist Block, the Koran to the Muslim world, Shakespeare is to Anglo-Saxon Australia.

This bronze group by the sculptor Bertram Mckennal, completed in 1926, shows Shakespeare, pen at the ready, surrounded by a few of his created companions — Hamlet (thoughtful), Falstaff (fat), Portia (as a boy), and Romeo and Juliet (embracing).

The Library of New South Wales, across, the road has a Shakespeare Memorial Library containing over 2,000 volumes; among them is a 1623 First Folio Edition of his works, and a First Edition of the tragedy of *Julius Caesar*.

⏹10⏹ The State Library of New South Wales

The library, with its classical portico facing the Royal Botanic Gardens, and its stately flight of steps, contains the world's greatest collection of Australiana. The building also houses spacious new exhibition galleries, a reading room of rare books, copying services, and video links with libraries throughout the State.

Its lobby is both imposing and simple. The marble floor was decorated by the Sydney mosaic artists the Melocco Brothers, incorporating Abel Tasman's seventeenth century map of New Holland (the continent's original name).

An Act of Parliament in 1879 required that a copy of every book printed and published in New South Wales should be lodged in the Library. This wise provision has made the Australian section of the Library an invaluable collection, and the building now contains over 140 kilometres of shelving.

The reading room — 50 metres (162½ feet) long and 26 metres (84½ feet) wide, and lined with galleries and micro-computer equipment, is one of Sydney's well-known sights. A special tunnel links this part of the library with the rest of the building.

The library's oldest wing, designed by John Horbury Hunt, was built to house the priceless 61,000-item Australiana collection donated by a wealthy Sydney recluse, David Scott Mitchell. This benefactor had devoted his life to spending his family's fortune on books, maps, paintings and manuscripts of Australia's past. Amongst the treasures he had amassed during his obsessive life were the original journals of both Captain James Cook (the explorer who discovered Botany Bay — *see story*) and Joseph Banks (the botanist who recommended to the British Government that Botany Bay be colonised with convicts).

The Mitchell Wing also contains the log book of Captain (later Governor) Bligh's *Bounty* (describing the infamous mutiny) and valuable manuscripts relating to the seventeenth century Pacific explorations of the Dutchman Abel Tasman (after whom the island state of Tasmania is named); as well as the log books of the Iberian navigators de Quiros and Torres, in search of the Great South Land.

The Shakespeare room contains a Latin book printed in 1472, a copy of the plays of English dramatist and poet Ben Jonson (dated 1616), and a first edition of the theatre of Beaumont and Fletcher.

The Mitchell Wing of the State Library of New South Wales

In 1929 the Government built the Dixson Wing to house the collection of maps, coins, portraits and memorabilia of early Australian settlement and life in the Pacific amassed by another shy bachelor collector, Sir William Dixson. Sir William also erected the library's three large bronze doors, in memory of David Scott Mitchell. (The panels show scenes from the lives of Aboriginals and Australian explorers.)

The Mitchell Wing is directly linked by covered walkways to the more modern General Reference Library in Macquarie Street, which offers a large number of facilities to readers, including 11 storeys of information (7 below-ground), and access to nearly 2 million items.

'Pointing the Bone', panel from the three bronze Library doors. Aboriginals often practiced the ritual of pointing a bone. Its aim was to cause the slow, painful death of an enemy, or of someone who broke the tribal law

11 Monuments to Bourke and Flinders

Standing outside the State Library in Shakespeare Place, is the oldest statue in Australia — representing Richard Bourke, Governor of the Colony from 1831-37. Unveiled before a large enthusiastic crowd on 11 April 1842, the statue sculpted by E. H. Baily bears a long inscription to this popular public figure (who introduced reforms such as trial-by-jury and increased religious tolerance, and laid the foundations of the city of Melbourne).

On a pedestal around the corner, on the Macquarie Street side of the library, stands W. R. Colton's bronze statue of the sea-explorer Matthew Flinders. From the moment he arrived in Sydney in 1795, Flinders resolved to investigate the east coast of New South Wales and Victoria. He accomplished this in a small boat called *Tom Thumb*, accompanied by the British surgeon George Bass. Their gallant journey was to open up the entire region to settlement.

In 1801, aboard the *Investigator*, Flinders became the first man to circumnavigate the continent. In a book he later wrote about his journeys, he was the first to use the name 'Australia' in regular writings — rather than the continent's older name of 'New Holland'. The word Australia, of course, was a corruption of 'Austrialia', the designation first used in 1606 by the explorer de Torres for the north of the continent, in honour of Phillip III of Austria.

Governor Bourke's statue paid for by Sydney's citizens

The oldest Parliament building in the world

South of the State Library along Macquarie Street stands the Parliament House of the State of New South Wales — the oldest continuously used parliamentary building in the world. Its central portion was built by convicts in the 1810s as part of Sydney Hospital, and it was first used as a Parliament in 1829.

A monument to its creator, Governor Macquarie (1761-1824), has been raised across the street outside an office building. Sculpted by John Dowie in 1973, the statue depicts Lachlan Macquarie, harried and windswept, the embodiment of Plutarch's dictum: 'He who is fond of building will soon ruin himself without the help of enemies.'

With its tapering columns, shuttered windows and panelled doors the design of Parliament House is typical of colonial Georgian architecture. (The Mint Museum, a southern wing of the same old Hospital also remains — a short distance further along the street.)

Entrance to State Parliament

A modern 14 storey building for politicians and staff is positioned behind the original building, facing the Domain and linked to Parliament House by a central circular courtyard with fountain.

As the Upper House, the Legislative Council (following the British tradition for the House of Lords) is dressed in red. The Legislative Assembly, (modelled on the British House of Commons) is correspondingly dressed in green. Its members are elected by popular vote every three years.

The Legislative Council and Assembly, and the Parliamentary Library, may be visited after application to the Usher of the Black Rod. When the Houses are in session visitors can listen to the proceedings from the public galleries.

Several permanent exhibitions are also open to the public.

Interior of State Parliament

13 The Little Boar and Sydney Hospital

The Little Boar (or, as it is known by its Italian name, *Il porcellino*) stands outside the Sydney Hospital in Macquarie Street. The statue is a replica of the fifteenth century sculpture that stands in the Florence haymarket in Italy, and is equally popular here in Sydney. It is said that if you rub its nose, the *little boar will grant you a wish*.

Sydney Hospital, behind it, was erected early in the last century as a hospital for convicts. The original building was 100 metres (325 feet) long, two stories high and enclosed by a massive wall similar to the one surrounding the Old Darlinghurst Gaol. The complex had been built by two enterprising Sydney citizens, Blaxcell and Riley, in return for the right to import 180,000 litres of rum into the colony, and thereafter came to be known as the *Rum Hospital*.

(Soon after the foundation of Sydney, rum and most other forms of alcohol became grimly important commodities. Convicts, officers, and soldiers were similarly dependent on drink. The use and sale of alcohol consequently affected every part of the colony's life — even its architecture and politics.)

Conditions in the hospital were alarming. The patients cooked their own food, the kitchen store rooms were used as morgues, there was no separation of the sexes, cripples were employed as nurses, and the surgeons did their operating wherever they found an available corner.

The hospital's first era ended in 1845 when enforced transportation from Britain ceased. In 1868 the first trained sisters arrived. In 1879 the centre block of the Rum Hospital was demolished to make way for the present structure. Designed by Thomas Rowe, the building has a grand staircase and lovely stained-glass windows. The plan for the nurses' wing at the rear had been suggested by Florence Nightingale. The two remaining wings of the *Rum Hospital* still stand today as the Old Mint Building and the State Parliament House.

Top: Il Porcellino on Macquarie Street

Bottom: View of Sydney Hospital from Martin Place

The Old Mint Museum

Originally part of an 1812 convict hospital, the Mint on Macquarie Street, is a two floor rectangular building made up of walls nearly a metre thick and surrounded on all sides by shaded verandahs. Over the years the building has had varied uses. Its two tiers of columns are made of cedar timber in the style of Doric mouldings, and are angled inwards in imitation of the optical illusions used in the Parthenon in Athens.

The building was designed by Governor Macquarie, with the aid of an architectural encyclopedia and ideas about life in a hot climate he had picked up in India. Construction was financed by local businessmen in exchange for permission to import a shipment of rum. (At the time this was a most precious item — 8 litres of rum could buy another man's wife.)

When the building was completed, architect Francis Greenway (newly transported from England) predicted its imminent collapse. However, 175 years later it is still standing, and houses a museum of the country's early decorative arts, as well as displays of coins, stamps and flags and exhibitions of colonial Australian life.

The Mint's colonnade along Macquarie Street

15 Hyde Park Prison Barracks

Until the year 1817, Sydney did not have prisons as such: the entire Australian continent was one *big* prison. Inmates were turned loose at the end of each day and left to fend for themselves for the night. Macquarie, the Governor of the period, held this to be the major contributing factor to the high crime rate, and consequently gave priority to the construction of a barracks to house the convicts at the northern end of Hyde Park.

Built by Francis Greenway — whose portrait may be seen on the ten-dollar note — the resulting prison barracks is a fine Georgian building of red sandstone brick and locally-produced timber. Classic in proportion, with Palladian bays and plain pilasters, it also features a symbolic Masonic 'triangle and eye' in the form of a pediment and early colonial clock (still wound once a week, by hand).

Inside, 1,000 prisoners once slept crowded together in hammocks less than a metre apart. Similar hammocks and other historical objects can be seen today in the building's exhibitions of early Sydney life, reconstructing what it was like to be a convict in Sydney 175 years ago. Exhibits also survey two centuries of Australian social life.

Queen's Square

In the open space at the southern end of Macquarie Street (known as Queen's Square) stands the fairy-godmother-like statue of Queen Victoria — made by the Hungarian sculptor J. E. Boehm in 1888. Opposite her, beside the Hyde Park Prison Barracks, stands her German husband Prince Albert The Good (called 'the good' to disguise his unpopularity) — cast by the English sculptor William Theed in 1866.

During the turbulent 1890s, when the British Empire was not very well liked in spite of all its achievements, Queen's Square was a place for volatile public meetings. The speakers stood on Queen Victoria's pedestal to address the crowds — many among them demanding that Australia become a republic, and making rude remarks about their Queen, who by then had ruled for 60 years.

17 St. James' Church

Situated in the heart of the legal district, this building (once meant to be a court-house) is at the upper end of King Street. Viewed from Queen's Square it certainly appears as the sober Georgian monument to godliness which it was intended to be; viewed from the Hunter Street end of Phillip Street, the Church offers one of the most charming and historically romantic architectural views in Sydney.

It was built between 1819 and 1822 by the convict-architect Francis Greenway, who produced an architectural gem of simplicity and chaste design. Made of local materials, the walls have double brick arches, multi-paned glass windows and classically inspired stone porticoes. The spire over its square brick tower was erected in 1824 and served for years as a landmark for ships in Sydney Harbour. The porches with vestries were added by John Verge in 1834, and are in the nature of Greenway's style. In 1894 Varney Parkes made substantial alterations to the interior, adding a semicircular sanctuary and replacing the old copper roof, which had been marked with bright arrows to prevent its theft.

The Church contains memorials to a number of renowned men and women. Among these are Alexander Macleay (founder of the Australian Museum), and explorers Edmund Kennedy, Aboriginal Jacky Jacky, and John Gilbert. Beneath, the Church a crypt originally meant to hold prisoners awaiting trial.

View of St James and Supreme Court from King Street

St. Mary's Cathedral

The Catholic church in Australia had difficult beginnings. Catholicism being banned in Sydney until 1820, Catholic convicts were forced to attend Protestant services under severe punishment. The religion was seen as a danger by the Protestant authorities, being the religion of the rebellious Irish who made up a large number of the Colony's population.

Situated at the eastern limits of the City, the Cathedral is the sixth largest in the world, and one of the finest examples of Gothic Revival architecture built in modern times. Erected in several stages between 1868 and 1928, in the local Pyrmont stone, the Cathedral features pointed arches, flying buttresses and ribbed vaults. The effect created by architect William Wardell is one of lightness and space.

St Mary's is a majestic edifice from any vantage point. With Hyde Park as its western-side garden, and the bronze statues of Cardinal Moran and Archbishop Kelly (by Bertram Mckennal) flanking the 37 steps leading to its main entrance, this cathedral on College Street is a notable Sydney landmark.

The building ranges north to south, with the choir pointing northwards. The western facade, modelled on Paris's Notre Dame, dominates College Street and Hyde Park. The entire length of the Cathedral is 106 metres, while its width across the nave and aisles is 24 metres. The central tower or lantern has a clear interior height from the building's floor of 30 metres (98 feet). The two towers above the grand southern entrance are each 46 metres (150 feet) high — the spires, which will take the towers to a height of over 100 metres (325 feet) have not yet been built. The design of the whole pile is grandiose yet sober.

Looking down the nave of the Cathedral to the High Altar, one is impressed by the lofty columns and arches, the carved clerestory and marble centre aisle; also of interest are the carved pulpit at the transept, and the wood-groined ceiling of the Sanctuary. The massive High Altar and the sculpture at its back (carved from New Zealand *oamaru* stone) are notable features. Measuring 23 metres (75 feet) by 12 metres (39 feet), the Sanctuary's mosaic is one of the finest achievements of the whole Cathedral.

Above the altar, the great northern window depicts the *Coronation of Our Lady in Heaven*. The western rose window has the Messiah as its central figure, with the principal figures of the Old Testament grouped around in two circles. The Crucifixion is situated on the east wall of the eastern transept and represents

St Mary's Cathedral with Lands Titles building on the left and the Domain in the background

Above: The Crucifixion on the east wall of the eastern transept

Right: The Crypt beneath the Cathedral. The mosaic decoration of the floor is in the form of a huge celtic cross, showing the six days of creation.

Christ on the cross with an angel catching the blood in the Holy Grail.

The eastern rose window represents (in the centre) Christ as a teacher, surrounded by St Paul and the Evangelists. Placed under the eastern rose window is the stained-glass of *Our Lady Help of Christians*, Patroness of Australia. This is a five-light window also portraying Irish saints. Along the eastern side aisle is the Baptistry, the carved-marble base and beaten-silver baptismal font being viewed through a brass grille and doors.

Tragically, the first Cathedral of St Mary's (raised on the same site) was destroyed by a fire in the last century. This fire and several other events are all depicted in the Cathedral windows along the western wall.

Commemorating the church's difficult inception (and including a representation of Governor Lachlan Macquarie — a Mason — laying the foundation stone of the first catholic church in Australia) is a series of stained-glass historical windows.

The crypt is an artless, vaulted structure, 46 metres (150 feet) by 26 metres (85 feet), with heavy arches spanning between column supports which then continue through the floor to become the arcade of the nave of the Church above. The crypt's floor is a large multicoloured mosaic decoration by Peter Melocco. Resting here are the five earlier Archbishops of Sydney — Polding, Vaughan, Moran, Kelly and Gilroy — and some of the pioneers of Catholicism in Australia.

The fountain with the goddess Diana in the foreground

19 The Archibald Fountain

A favourite meeting place for friends and lovers, the Fountain is situated in Hyde Park near Queen's Square and St Mary's Cathedral. Financed by J.F. Archibald and designed in the classical style by the French sculptor François Sicard in 1933, the Fountain shows the god Apollo at the centre of a group of mythological figures pertaining strong symbolic relation to the history and future of Australia.

The Apollo figure, standing about 2.5 metres (8 feet) high, stretches out his right arm while holding a lyre in his left hand. Symbolising the spirit of the young sun-drenched Australia he points the way to the sea — and the future. Radiating behind him, jets of spraying water represent the rays of the sun as he looks eastwards, watching the cycle of the rising and setting sun.

Below him, the hunting goddess Diana represents Australia's pioneers. Pan, the god of nature, a ewe and a ram at his side, represents the pastoralists who introduced sheep and wool as a source of wealth to this country. The Greek hero Theseus, vanquishing the half-man/half-bull Minotaur, symbolises the heroic tamers of this vast wild continent. Frolicking between these figures dolphins spurt jets of water.

The Great Synagogue

On the city side of Hyde Park — in Elizabeth Street, between Park and Market Streets — is the stone-arch building of the Great Synagogue. The best-known Jewish building in Australia, it was designed by Thomas Rowe (architect of Sydney Hospital), in a combination of Byzantine and Gothic styles, and erected in 1873 to accommodate the congregations of two previously existing synagogues in York and Macquarie Streets.

The towers of the building are of Pyrmont sandstone, moulded and carved in the elaborate manner of Victorian Baroque; the intricate wheel window is decorated with traditional motifs; the cast iron columns and groined-ceiling of the interior create a feeling of lightness.

The Ark — situated at the end of the building, closest to Jerusalem — contains ancient, hand-written scrolls of the five books of Moses. Above the Ark 'is the Choir Gallery, surmounted by a dome with small, circular stained-glass windows. The ceiling is covered in gold stars symbolising the world's creation.

21 Sandringham Gardens

In the northern half of Hyde Park, at the corner of Park and College Streets, is the Sandringham Garden, built to the memory of Kings George V and VI. A formal amphitheatre-shaped garden, it has a fountain at the centre, and a floor decorated with Aboriginal motifs in ochres and reds. The flower beds, planted with annuals, present a most appealing sight in bloom.

The garden at the corner of Park and College Streets

22 Monument to Captain Cook

Hyde Park was initially Sydney's Common, or 'Exercising Ground'. Later it became the site of the first race-meeting to be held in the colony. Later still, when Governor Bourke's water conduit from Centennial Park became functional, it was the gathering place of the carts used to take fresh water around town.

In the southern corner, bounded by Park and College Streets and opposite the Ausralian Museum, hides the statue of Captain James Cook (1728-1779) — the city's sole memorial to the man who claimed Australia as territory for the British *(see story Australia's Birthplace)*. Cook, one of the greater navigator-explorers, sailed the world's oceans several times in the service of King George III. Unhappily, nine years after charting the east coast of Australia, he was slain and eaten by Sandwich Island (Hawaiian) cannibals.

Cook — worthy successor to Columbus and Magellan — seems to greet the visitor with a hearty welcome. Indeed he appears so delighted on his granite pedestal — so eager to show off the results of his discovery — that one can't fail to ponder for a moment the rapid progress Sydney has made in the 200 years since this man sighted the first landing place in Botany Bay. *(See story)*.

This statue, sculpted by Thomas Woolner in 1879, was funded by concerts in the Hyde Park Pavilion which stood on the same ground last century. At the time the Pavilion was one of the largest wooden buildings in the world, with a ballroom 77 metres (250 feet) long, fountains spraying perfumes, walls furnished in crimson-and-white satin and a royal box to welcome Australia's first visiting Royalty, Queen Victoria's son, Prince Alfred.

Captain Cook in Hyde Park, opposite the Australian Museum

23 The Anzac War Memorial

Since 1885, Australian troops have taken part in wars in East Africa, South Africa, China, Europe, the Middle East, North Africa, the South Pacific, the Far East and South East Asia. Their struggles and sacrifices are remembered in a melancholic shrine in the southern half of Hyde Park, near the start of Oxford Street.

The noble Anzac War Memorial is placed at the end of an avenue of trees which extends from Macquarie Street, past the Archibald Fountain and down the length of Hyde Park. Erected in 1934 — as Hitler, Mussolini and Stalin were sowing the seeds of the next world war — the building was the creation of the Australian painter and architect Bruce Dellitt.

Taking the form of a stepped geometric Art Deco tower, the Memorial is covered in pink granite and stands 30 metres (97.5 feet) tall on a podium 46 metres (149 feet) long by 27 metres (88 feet) wide. The outstanding feature of the exterior is its 16 buttresses. They are surmounted by the granite figures of soldiers representing all units of the Australian Army, seated, heads bowed in respect and sadness. On the northern side is the Pool of Reflection, where the visitor can contemplate peace and the wastefulness of war.

Dominating the interior are the Hall of Memory and the Hall of Silence immediately below it. Here, placed so as to compel all entering the Hall of Memory to gaze down upon it, is a central sculpture symbolising 'Sacrifice': a naked soldier is borne aloft on a shield supported by his mother, sister, wife and child. There is no pomp or glamour in this group — it tells of that noblest human quality — self-sacrifice for duty.

Above the visitor rises the domed ceiling studded with 120,000 gold stars — one for every Australian who enlisted in World War One. The sculptures, external and internal, are by George Rayner Hoff, who was born on the Isle of Man, served in the British Army in the First World War and later taught art in Sydney. Staged on the ground floor of the Memorial is a permanent photographic exhibition commemorating Australia's participation in nine armed invasions of foreign territories.

Every Thursday just before 1 pm the Army mounts a ceremonial Guard of Honour which marches from this Memorial to the Cenotaph for the War Dead, in Martin Place.

The Memorial dedicated to the Anzacs, (an acronym for Australian New Zealand Army Corps), who first fought together in 1915 during World War One

The Australian Museum

Founded in 1827, the Museum's earliest collections were kept in Parliament House, and transferred to the present building in 1849. The original building was designed by Mortimer Lewis and is contained within the walls of the present Museum. The Palladio-style frontage to College Street and its 12 metre (40 feet) pillars are the work of James Barnet.

Continually enlarged over the years, the museum specialises in Australian zoology, mineralogy, anthropology and palaeontology. Among some wonderful exhibits are a giant prehistoric wombat and a sperm whale skeleton 15 metres (55 feet) long. The botanical specimens of the Museum are housed in the Herbarium at the Royal Botanic Gardens *(see story)*. The Museum has three levels.

Facade of the Australian Museum overlooking Hyde Park South

Ground Level:

Aboriginal Australia. An exhibition devoted to the way-of-life of the country's Aboriginals. The Aboriginal people came from South-East Asia some 40,000 years ago. The exhibition features bark paintings, funeral poles, bark canoes and reconstructed camp sites, with explanations of the main features of Aboriginal history.

Papua New Guinea. The island to the north of Australia has a fascinating variety of cultures, languages and people. This exhibition focuses on the life of the Apangai village on the Sepik River. Museum scientists have documented the village rituals and re-created the interior of a spirit house. There are also details of a yam-based society, where the man who grows the largest yam (a type of sweet potato) receives the greatest respect.

Australian Mammals. Australia's unique marsupials — kangaroos, ringtail possums, wombats, koalas and the rare Tasmanian wolf (*Thylacine*).

Level One:

Hall of Minerals. A display of Australia's rich array of rocks and minerals. Models of quartz crystals; examples of unusual opals; minerals found in caves and salt lakes; volcanic deposits.

Level Two:

Marine Hall. An insight into the three oceans surrounding the continent and the habits of its dangerous creatures including the blue ringed octopus, the blue bottle and the various sharks. The exhibition also seeks to explain the forces of the deep as well as the mysteries of wave formation and tidal waves.

Discovery Room. A gallery for all ages on the different areas of natural or cultural science, with exciting 'hands-on' exhibits which can be touched, explored and studied.

Tracks through Time. The exhibits in this hall take a look at the origins of humankind through the ages. The arrival of *homo sapiens*, the first humans, on Australian soil. A study of prehistoric Aboriginal life.

Rituals. A gallery about the human life cycle as experienced in different cultures. Each section covers a particular stage of life from birth to death, with examples of various Pacific, African and Indian societies.

Australian Environment. Illustrating the changing environment over the last 200,000 years with stress on the crucial events surrounding the arrival of the Europeans.

Fossils. The history of life on earth as inscribed in the fossilised remains of plants and animals found in Australia. The fossil of a 370-million-year-old air-breathing fish found in Sydney; traces

Tyrannosaurus Rex at play. Some of the world's most important Dinosaur finds have been made in Australia

of the oldest-known back-boned animal (found in 480-million-year-old rocks in Central Australia); the remains of the dinosaurs *Tyrannosaurus, Stegosaurus*, and *Archaeopteryx* (the oldest known bird).

Birds and Insects. An exhibition of the abundant bird life of Australia, the uniqueness of emus, cockatoos, lyrebirds, honey eaters and parrots; also featured are butterflies from the tropics; on special screen precuts films on how a variety of creatures live and depend on each other for survival.

Entrance to the hall of 'Aboriginal Australia'

25 | St Andrew's Cathedral

This, the oldest cathedral in Australia, is a Gothic revival building in what is known as the 'perpendicular style'. It has a nave, choir, and sacrarium, and north and south transepts. There are two towers at the west end of the nave. Within its walls the building is 49 metres (159 feet) long by 19 metres (62 feet) wide; its transept is 39 metres (127 feet) by 4.5 metres (127 feet). Although comparatively small in dimensions, St Andrew's nevertheless compares favourably with many of the English cathedrals.

The building has 26 stained-glass windows made by Hardman of Birmingham, financed by the donations of various nineteenth century parishioners. The windows on the south side represent the miracles of Christ, while the northern windows illustrate Biblical Parables. There are also windows on the transfiguration of Christ, his Baptism, the Last Supper, and the Resurrection. The great east window shows the life of St Andrew.

The Cathedral also contains a replica of the tomb of the Bishop of Broughton — the only prelate in history to bear the designation 'prelate of Australia' — (see the story on the Garrison Church) — and whose remains are buried in Canterbury Cathedral (the first post-Reformation bishop to be so honoured). His home, Tusculum, may be visited in Kings Cross. Nearby his memorial is a copy of the *Great Bible* of 1538 — ordered by Thomas Cromwell in 1539 — this copy was presented to the Cathedral after being found in an old chest in Northamptonshire, England.

The Cathedral's history dates as far back as August 1819, when the original foundation stone was laid by Governor Lachlan Macquarie. Little or no progress was made for the next two decades, when Governor Richard Bourke had the walls erected to their proper height, but the building remained unroofed for years. In 1860, Bishop Barker succeeded in raising sufficient funds for the completion of the edifice, and the Cathedral was consecrated on St Andrew's Day, 30 November 1868.

The building's final architect Edmund Blacket, and his wife are also buried here. The two towers he designed (away from the George Street side) are based on St Mary's Church in Oxford, Great Britain, and are counted among his finest works. Blacket had them face west in the traditional manner. It was not until 1949 that it was finally accepted that the Cathedral gave onto a back lane (incorporated since then into Sydney Square) — a new entrance and a small porch were then provided on the George Street side, by architect Leslie Wilkinson. To appreciate Blacket's original concept, it is therefore worthwhile walking round to the western facade.

On the northern inside wall of the Cathedral hangs a Union Jack which was saved by an Australian prisoner-of-war during World War Two. He carried it in Singapore, Burma and Japan — where it was flown on V.J. (Victory in Japan) Day 1945 after the taking down of the Japanese flag. Placed in the wall near Blacket's tomb, are stones from ancient British cathedrals and the House of Commons, and House of Lords in London. The pavement of the chapel sanctuary (also on the north side of the Cathedral) is made of marble from St Paul's Cathedral, and was laid in 1953.

St Andrew's style is Low Church simplicity.

The Cathedral's western towers seen from Sydney Square. Much of original Sydney was designed to face west. The door below the towers is no longer in use

Sydney Town Hall

This grand Victorian building stands next to St Andrew's Cathedral in George Street on ground which was once a public cemetery. The ornate and roomy edifice is the heritage of the 1870s, a tumultuous period in the city's history — when Sydney was a seaport of 288,000 people offering 3,167 pubs (taverns) for its alcohol-loving inhabitants.

It was also a time when aggressive men with big appetites and big ideas, (many of whom had become rich from criminal enterprises) dreamt of uniting the continent into a nation — while at the same time a ten-year-old boy could be sentenced to a flogging of 18 lashes for picking a flower or writing a naughty word on a wall.

The building's foundation stone was laid in 1868 by Queen Victoria's son, the Duke of Edinburgh, whose visit to Sydney was the first by a member of the British Royal Family. (The Duke was just recovering from an assassination attempt made on his life earlier in the visit by a fanatical Irishman called Henry O'Farrell, whose brother had already attempted to assassinate a Catholic Archbishop.)

At least eight architects had a hand in the making of the Town Hall, as its design changed over the years. The general style is Victorian Baroque. The building is 57 metres (185 feet) wide and 95 metres (309 feet) long. The Clock Tower, traditionally one of Sydney's outstanding landmarks but now transcended by the buildings around it, was completed in 1881. It stands 55 metres (179 feet) in height to the top of the finial.

The Central Entrance Hall is decorated in moulded plaster work, with marble floors and baronial stained-glass windows depicting moments in Australia's history. The Main Hall (Concert Hall), the venue for some of the world's great musicians, was built in 1888 and seats 2,300 persons. The Town Hall Grand Organ is one of the largest and most powerful in the world, with 6 keyboards, 127 stops, and 8,672 pipes varying from 1 centimetre to 20 metres in length.

Situated in George Street, on ground that was once a consecrated cemetery, the Town Hall has been the focal point of municipal politics for well over a hundred years. The Sydney Square side features the famous 'winking lion''. Curiously, though Sydney ceased to be a 'town' long ago, the building's name was never changed to City Hall

27 The Queen Victoria Building

In 1810, Governor Macquarie ordered that the space bounded by George, Druitt, York and Market Streets be turned into a market area. Sheds were erected and country people brought their produce there in wagons or boats from the farming districts outside Sydney.

Years later, in 1889, the City demolished the sheds and called for the design of a 201-metre-long (653 feet) and 25-metre-wide (81 feet) municipal market building. The resulting structure, named the Queen Victoria Building, became one of the City's most ornate, and took its architect George McRae five years to complete.

The QVB, as it is known, features rose-coloured stained-glass windows, a glass barrel vault skylight, a 3-metre-high clock in the shape of a castle, and 21 copper-covered domes (the largest is 20 metres in diameter and scales 58 metres above the pavement).

Inside, the building houses 200 stylish shops on three open levels, a grand basalt staircase, and a marble pavement of more than one million tiles.

Placed before the entrance is the seated statue of Queen Victoria. Victoria, who felt that her public image ought to be forever serious, forbade any laughing or smiling portraits of herself. She likewise ordered that all monuments must portray her as a severe figure, conveying a caring Monarch contemplating the lives of her subjects.

Right: The building's facade along George Street

Queen Victoria's seated statue overlooks the city centre. Behind the Monarch is a memorial to one of her small dogs

28 | Sydney Tower

Visible from any part of the city, the Sydney Tower rises from Market Street to a height of 304.8 metres (1,000 feet), offering grand 360-degree views from the Pacific Ocean eastwards, to the Blue Mountains in the west.

Three double-decker lifts (connected by video cameras) take visitors to the golden turret's observation decks. Designed by Sydney architect Donald Crone, the tower is supported by a bouquet of 56 cables, each weighing 7 tonnes. The shaft, 7 metres (23 feet) in diameter, was constructed in prefabricated steel units bolted together; unusual slots designed into the shaft allow the wind to move through it at high speeds.

The turret has 9 levels, four of them open to the public. On Level 7, a large water tank acts as a pendulum — when wind hits the tower, the tank moves in the opposite direction helping to stabilise the building.

29 | MLC Centre at Martin Place

Proudly penetrating the sky at Martin Place is the MLC Centre. The creation of architect Harry Seidler, this is a 68-storey reinforced concrete structure, 226 metres (740 feet) high, invoking the work of the Italian architect Nervi. The Yellow 'S'- sculpture on the top plaza is by Charles Perry as is the hanging bronze Mercator in the theatre lobby beneath the building. The centre has a plaza, with two floors of shops and restaurants and terrace tables; the incorporated Theatre Royal seats 1,100 — its entrance is from King Street.

30 | Australia Tower and Square

Sydney's first modern skyscraper, Australia Tower (again designed by Harry Seidler) rises above George and Bond Streets, Built in 1967, in an idealised Renaissance style, it is a 50-storey, 20-sided polygon, 41 metres in diameter and 171 metres high. A special lift travels to an observation deck, offering vistas of the entire city. Australia Square below, bounded by Pitt and Bond Streets, recreates in the same way as the Italian town squares the combination of protective environment, sunlight and good food, inviting people to relax, eat, drink and enjoy themselves.

In Bond Street opposite, is the Sydney Stock Exchange, with a viewing gallery for visitors.

Sydney Tower seen from the bottom of William Street

The MLC Tower seen from Martin Place. The Commercial Travellers'
Association building is in the foreground

The painter Dobell's memorial obelisk in Martin Place

Martin Place is an urban pedestrian plaza stretching from Macquarie Street opposite Sydney Hospital, to George Street. It features fountains, sculptures, an open-air amphitheatre, a colonnade on the side of the General Post Office, flower-sellers, international-newspaper vendors, a tourist information kiosk and a station to Sydney's underground railway. It is the city's banking centre.

The Cenotaph at the George Street end was designed by the sculptor Bertram Mackennal in memory of the soldiers of World War One. The geometric obelisk of silver cubes, near Pitt Street, is by Bert Flugelman — erected in 1979, it commemorates the Australian painter William Dobell.

Circular Quay (Sydney Cove)

Arriving at Sydney Cove in 1788, the British established themselves at today's Circular Quay. Two hundred years ago, this was a bay of small beaches and ragged shores. Phillip, the colony's first governor, named the place Sydney Cove in honour of his politician patron in London — the city thus acquiring its name.

As the years passed, however, it was decided to amend the ragged shores of the Cove to an even horseshoe-shape worthy of a maritime city. Rubble from the Argyle Cut (see *story*) and sandstone from the Harbour islands were consequently used to fill in the cove, under the direction of architect Mortimer Lewis. The subsequent formation of Circular Quay and reclamation of 4 hectares (10 acres) of mudflats behind the sea-wall took 7 years — and the toil of thousands of convicts.

There were about 27,000 prisoners in New South Wales at the time of the Quay's construction, 24,000 of them male — beings who were abused and brutalised in the filthiest medieval manner, while Europe glittered in its cocoon of 'progressive sophistication'.

As yet, no worthy monument has been erected to the unsung heroes of that era who endured unimaginable suffering and penalty to lay the foundations for Australia's rapid development.

Circular Quay is their living memorial.

View of Circular Quay from the Overseas Terminal. The ferry jetties are in the foreground; the Cahill Highway and the city train service run above the Quay;

Old Customs House

This building faces Circular Quay on the spot where, according to tradition, the British set up camp soon after landing in 1788. The building was begun in the 1840s but underwent a series of changes as Sydney became more prosperous and her Controllers of Customs accumulated more bribes. Macquarie, Darling and other governors attempted to stem this corruption, but their efforts were fruitless.

Some customs chiefs went to great lengths of publicly demonstrating their innocence. When Captain John Piper (Point Piper is named after him) was suspended as Controller of Customs for allowing merchants to pay duty on credit, he had himself rowed out to the harbour entrance, to dispatch himself into what he prophesied as a 'watery grave'. (The good Captain's servants, however, rescued him.)

Robert Paton's Lion and Unicorn sculpture which surmounts the portico of Customs House, is a favourite Sydney artwork and is much admired and reproduced. At the side of the building, in Loftus Street, is the spot where Governor Phillip first raised the British flag up a gum-tree in 1788. 100 metres further up, in Macquarie Place, are the remains of his ship *Sirius*.

Customs House — its pillars hide the original building

33 Cadman's Cottage

Built about the time Napoleon was preparing for his final showdown, this little building has a great significance to Australians. The oldest dwelling in Sydney, it was built by convicts using primitive tools and inhabited soon after by the Governor's boat crew.

In 1816 the crew acquired a new chief, John Cadman, who had journeyed to Australia as a convict in 1798. As supervisor of the Rowboat Guard, his job was to ferry the Governor around the Harbour and up the Parramatta River to the Old Government House.

When not using his boats for this purpose he hauled them up before the entrance to the house. To the visitor standing before the building in the middle of George Street, this would seem odd. In Cadman's day, however, the ocean came right up to the cottage and a small beach lay where the street is now.

Following the land reclamations of the mid 1800s, the cottage was used by different people. Several famous murders took place here during the nineteenth century. Cadman's Cottage was also the site of the first meeting of Freemasons in Australia.

The cottage seen from George Street on the outskirts of the Rocks area. To the right the boat-house annex, in the background Circular Quay

Dutch Gable House

The Australasian Steam Navigation Company Headquarters, (also called Dutch Gable House) was erected at Circular Quay West in 1883. This genial building, designed by William Wardell (creator of St Mary's Cathedral), with its Dutch-Flemish gable roof, central tower, pyramid spire and observation platform was for years used for sighting incoming ships in advance of their docking, thus enabling importers to be at the wharves in time for the ships' arrival.

At the edge of The Rocks, just off George Street, the building overlooks the Overseas Terminal Plaza, the famous Campbell Warehouses (with their varied restaurants and shops and flamboyant sails), the local hotels, the Harbour Bridge and the Opera House across the Quay.

The ASNC building seen from Campbell's Cove

35 | Argyle Cut at the Rocks

Positioned at the top of the Rocks area in Argyle Street, this tunnel was hacked through solid rock. Work commenced in 1843 with convicts using hammers and chisels, the aim being to provide a short and direct route across the peninsula from Sydney Cove to Millers Point. The Government also wanted a road to by-pass the dangerous slums which had sprung up in the local area's meandering streets.

The Rocks, inhabited since the landing of the First Fleet, harboured the prostitutes, thieves, gamblers, and liquor traders of Sydney. Here also the colony's smugglers provided goods for the black market.

Progress on the Cut was slow since the labour force utilised the most primitive of hand tools and could work little faster despite the incentive of the lash. When the system of Convict Transportation ended and slave labour was no longer provided by Great Britain, the city was obliged to employ paid workmen — who eventually completed the Cut in 1867.

Today the Cut is surmounted by a concrete overpass leading to the Harbour Bridge. A set of nearby steps takes the visitor to the Southern Pylon Lookout and the Astronomical Observatory, while the road through the Cut itself arrives at the Garrison Church.

The Mining and Geological Museum at the edge of the Rocks

The Garrison Church

This home-spun old church of the Anglican denomination is found in the Rocks area — at the top of the hill near the Astronomical Observatory and the Argyle Cut.

Being the place of worship for the 50th British Queen's Own Regiment (until English Prime Minister Sir William Gladstone withdrew the Imperial troops from the Colony in 1870) the regimental crests and insignias can still be seen on the columns of the church's interior.

The church was built in the so-called *Early English Gothic*, on the orders of William Broughton — who was appointed 'Bishop of Australia' in 1836, thereby inheriting the largest diocese in the world (the Australian mainland, Tasmania and Norfolk Island).

Designed by Henry Ginn and originally destined for the Rocks' 'godless and sinful' mariners who Broughton aspired to save, the Church of the Holy Trinity (its real name) became a soldiers' church instead. Left, however, half-finished by Ginn, it had to be completed by the architect Edmund Blacket in 1879.

The church has two curious historical features: for years no collection plate was ever passed around (against the custom of Anglican churches), donations instead being taken at the door; and the church was never consecrated.

The Garrison Church and Argyle Cut at the top of the Rocks

37 The Astronomical Observatory

High above the Harbour on the Rocks area side of the city is one of the City's most pleasant places — Observatory Hill. Its huge, old Moreton Bay Fig trees, clear-day views of the Blue Mountains, and panoramas of the Western side of the harbour are typical Sydney attractions. Additionally the location has the historic Astronomical Observatory Museum.

Built in 1857, the Observatory's main tower was one of Sydney's best-known landmarks. From December 1858 a 'time-ball' signal gave the exact time to all the shipmasters in the harbour. At one o'clock daily the ball on the weather vane was dropped, and a gun was fired at Fort Denison (*see story*) in Sydney Harbour, indicating the correct time for setting clocks and watches.

In 1887, as part of a world-wide scheme, astronomers at the Observatory undertook to map 750,000 stars in about a fifteenth part of the southern sky. Despite difficulties this 'astrographic catalogue' was completed in 1962. Today the building is no longer a working observatory — other centres have been built at Mt Stromlo and Siding Springs — but in addition to the interesting daytime displays, nightly viewing of the southern sky is still available to the public.

Sydney Harbour Bridge

Work on the Bridge began in 1923, the first task being to excavate 14-metre-deep (45½ feet) sandstone beds on either side of the Harbour, and fill them with concrete. Four huge pylons 89 metres (289 feet) tall were built out of 42,672 tons (42,000 tonnes) of granite to anchor the crawler cranes used to hoist the bridge's steel panels into place. On average 1,400 men were employed in the operations, for nearly nine years. (This included the construction of elevated steel-and-concrete approaches at both ends.)

By 1928 the two halves of the arch began to creep out from the opposing shores. Great accuracy was required to keep the southern and the northern halves of the enormous structure aligned to within a centimetre. In 1931, with each half of the arch finished and rampant, both sets of side cables were slackened, a centimetre at a time — for according to calculations, when the halves met the arch would support itself.

On 15 August 1931, with a few centimetres remaining to be slackened, a 120 kilometre per hour gale struck the city. It continued to rampage throughout the night as all Sydney watched, fearful that the unjoined swaying arches might crash to the deep harbour waters below. The design (by Australian J.J.C. Bradfield and Englishman Sir Ralph Freeman) triumphed, however,and a few days later the workmen joined up what was then the world's largest steel arch: 134 metres (436 feet) in height with a 504 metre (1638 feet) span.

During the ensuing year work began on suspending the bridge's carriageway on steel hangers. This started in the centre, where the longest hangers of 58 metres (188 feet) were first raised from barges and then set into position. Thus was created the bridge's decking which, at a height of 52 metres (169 feet) above water, allowed what was then considered the largest of ocean liners to pass beneath. (The modern Cunard liner *Queen Elizabeth II* has only a metre to spare.)

Since its 1932 opening, the bridge, romantic and brooding, has attracted scores of suicides (some of whom have survived the jump), and numerous daredevil acrobats and various assorted thrill-seekers. It is constantly being flown under, scaled over, and festooned by humorists and protesters alike. All this time 160,00 vehicles pass over it daily, while above them workmen using 32,000 litres of paint take ten years to give the Bridge a new rust resistant coat.

Overleaf: The Harbour Bridge seen from Dawes Point. The Bridge rests mainly on four steel pins, each 35.5 centimetres (14 inches) in diametre and 4.16 metres (13 feet 8 inches) long

On hot days the arch's peak expands to an extra 20 centimetres as the bridge heats up and dilates. Despite this, the bridge is *not* the longest steel arch bridge in the world, though it *is* listed in the *Guinness Book of Records* as the *widest* with a deck of 49 metres (160 feet), incorporating 8 lanes of traffic, 2

railtracks and 2 footways.

The four pylons, despite appearances, do not support the bridge but have been left in place for storage and decoration. The southern pylon's 202 steps may be climbed for one of the best views of Sydney Harbour.

39 | Darling Harbour Square

Situated 400 metres from the centre of the City, at the western end of Market Street, the Darling Harbour complex spreads in a semi-circle around Cockle Bay. Conceived to suit the tropical environment, the area consists of the Sydney Aquarium, the National Maritime Museum, the Harbourside Marketplace, a Convention Centre, Exhibition and Entertainment Centres, and the exotic Chinese Gardens.

The Entertainment Centre at the southern end of the complex is Australia's largest auditorium, with a seating capacity of 12,000. It is a column-free building with a 50 metre (162 feet) wide arena, and contains enough concrete to have built a 1 metre (3 feet) wide path for a distance of 100 kilometres (60 miles).

The *Exhibition Centre* stands opposite the City, overlooking the main Darling Harbour plaza. Covering an area of 2.5 hectares (6¼ acres) (the equivalent of five football fields) it was designed by Philip Cox and has the largest exhibition space in Australia. Its roof is held in place by a system of 20 masts, each 38 metres (125 feet) tall. Inside, the five interlocking halls of the Centre have the height of a five storey building and can accommodate over 500 exhibitors. The external walls are made of tinted glass. Stepped back in five stages, the pleasing facade conveys the impression of a series of boats lying at anchor on the edge of the Harbour.

The *Convention Centre*, adjoined to the Exhibition Centre, is a seven storey building designed to hold meetings and conferences. Its main hall is an impressive 3,500 seat amphitheatre, accessed via lifts, escalators and a grand sweeping staircase. The Centre also contains 20 other meeting rooms and halls to accommodate between 80 and 700 people each. The southern entrance is paved in polished stone and opens onto a 2,500 square metre (22,500 square feet) gallery-reception area overlooking the waterfront promenade. The large terrace design is capable of holding an Australian-style barbecue for 1,000 visitors. By day, the glass eastern facade mirrors the city skyline. By night, the columns of the Centre gleam with intertwined spirals of light.

The Harbourside Marketplace is a two storey colonial style building 300 metres (975 feet) long, erected along the western side of the Cockle Bay Promenade. It houses 200 shops and 8 waterfront restaurants and terrace cafes. There is also a 600 seat tavern. Opposite the main entrance, in the central Crystal Galleria, rises a 9 metre (30 feet) tall sculpture by David

The Harbourside Marketplace on the shores of Darling Harbour.
Much of the land was reclaimed in the 1920s with rubble produced
by the tunneling of the City Underground

Humphries depicting six life-sized dolphins swimming in the company of a human around the blue and white globe of the Earth.

The National Maritime Museum, also designed in glass and steel by Philip Cox, houses Australia's collection of maritime history. The roof of the building rises in waves to a height of 38 metres (124 feet) while the structure itself extends for 100 metres (325 feet). Inside are displays on immigration by ship, the Royal Australian Navy, surfing, underwater diving, yacht racing and Australia's beach culture.

The fleet of ships exhibited in the 10 storey high building includes the 100 year old New Zealand *Akarana*; the pearl fishing boat *John Louis* from Broome in West Australia; the Vietnamese fishing boat *Hong Mai* which brought refugees to Australia; *HMAS Advance*, a patrol boat featured in a popular TV series; and a fragment of the ship which discovered Australia in 1770 — Captain James Cook's *Endeavour*.

The 22-metre-wide 'Wave Pool' outside the Convention Centre. Created by Robert R. Woodward, the water flows from the outside towards the centre across a sequence of steps, and creates a complex series of wave actions

The Sydney Aquarium

The main building, designed by architect Philip Cox, is shaped like a warehouse in homage to the corrugated-iron culture of Australia. The Aquarium encloses over 3,200 square metres (28,800 square feet) of exhibition space and presents 5,000 fish in a variety of habitats.

Within the Main Hall, exhibits display an array of local and tropical fish. Visitors can browse through coral gardens, view the secrets of tidal pools and follow a stream to the sea. There are displays of crocodiles, fish from the Great Barrier Reef, turtles and a variety of sea creatures.

Moored outside the main building are two large floating oceanarium tanks through which visitors travel under the sea in large acrylic tubes to view an abundance of marine life; 146 metres (476 feet) of moving walkways are incorporated into these two buildings.

Oceanarium 1, dedicated to the marine life of the open ocean, contains 1.25 million litres (275,000 gallons) of sea-water and is home to sharks such as the Port Jackson and the grey nurse. Among these swim stingrays and schools of large ocean fish.

Oceanarium 2 displays the marine life of the Harbour; 42 metres (136 feet) long by 22 metres (71.5 feet) wide, it contains 1.5 million litres (330,00 gallons) of water. On show are green moray eels, sea horses, lionfish and many other of the 570 marine species found in Sydney Harbour.

The Sydney Aquarium's two floating tanks, 40 metres long and 20 metres wide each. Ocean water pumped into the tanks is treated at the rate of 1,500 tonnes per hour to ensure maximum clarity

41 The Chinese Gardens

Positioned at the south-east end of Darling Harbour near the entrance to Chinatown, the Chinese Gardens cover an area of 10,000 square metres (32,500 square feet). Carefully crafted, this world-in-miniature is the only authentic Cantonese-style garden of such size outside mainland China.

Aiming to create a sensation of eternity, the gardens offer a chance to admire the ingenuity and artistry of a Taoist-inspired gardening philosophy nurtured over 25 centuries.

The visitor wanders a variety of paths uncertain as to where the garden ends. Each sight presents a balanced and framed picture of natural contrasting elements: narrow areas border unobstructed spaces; jagged rocks meet sleek waters; rounded edges encounter straight lines.

Central to the gardens is a rambling dainty watercourse. Two green granite lions guard the entrance, and a 'dragon' wall welcomes the visitor — the two dragons represent Canton (Guangzhou) and Sydney, juggling the pearl of dialectic prosperity between them.

A waterside pavilion and courtyard of repose are followed by a climb to a waterfall. At the highest point, a three-tiered pagoda is the focal site of the Garden — its yellow glazed roof, reserved only for imperial edifices, in sharp contrast with the garden's general commoner style.

The rock forest in the second stage of the Garden portrays the beauty of limestone; the boat-house further down creates the illusion of movement; while the tea-house, poised above lotus plants, brings the walk through the gardens to an enjoyable close.

The visitor is then free to wander the adjacent Darling Harbour Complex or the Chinatown area situated between Railway Square and Goulburn Street.

42 | The Powerhouse Museum

The Powerhouse is a branch of the Museum of Applied Arts and Sciences, dating from 1880. Situated behind the Darling Harbour Exhibition Centre on Harris Street, it is the largest museum in Australia. The 9,500 exhibits are spread over an area of 2.4 hectares (6 acres), with 25 simultaneous exhibitions devoted to the decorative arts, social history, science, and technology.

The massive domed entrance facing Harris Street is constructed of concrete, glass and steel, but with an 'Australian' style corrugated iron roof. The atrium is in the fashion of a nineteenth century railway station, topped by an arched roof built with a special steel bending technique. The lofty 'galleria', inspired by soaring gothic cathedrals, was created by architect Lionel Glendenning.

The Museum's core is composed of buildings once used to generate electricity for Sydney's public transport system, incorporating such Victorian buildings as the *Engine House* (1899), the *Turbine House* (1901) and the *Boiler House* (1901). Three levels of the complex are connected by banks of escalators, and in one section a glass lift takes visitors to the mezzanine-floor restaurant, allowing them to view each floor as they do so.

Some of the most captivating exhibits deal with science. There is an immense Boulton and Watt steam engine made in 1785, with a majestic 6 metre (19.5 feet) flywheel. Designed by James Watt and used by an English brewery for 100 years the engine has been restored to full working order. Also on show are 12 other steam engines, and the first railway engine made in New South Wales — *Locomotive No.1,* which ran the Sydney to Parramatta line from 1855. Visitors may board the train's carriage and experience through sound tapes the atmosphere of a day's outing in 1863.

The Powerhouse has what is claimed to be the largest suspended aerial object in any museum — the eight tonne World War Two Catalina flying boat *Frigate Bird II,* with a wingspan of 32 metres (104 feet). In 1951 the plane made a historic long distance flight to South America. Along with other aircraft, it soars above the *Transport* exhibits hung from the roof of the Boiler House. At the other end of the scale, the Museum's smallest object is a one-centimetre-high glass dog.

The exhibitions in *Decorative Arts* offer, a collection of Wedgwood china; *Recollections* presents a working 1889 model Strasbourg clock, while *The Information Machine* takes the visitor to the heart of a computer to make intelligible its workings; in *Space* there are displays of space habitation modules, a Soviet moon-rover and Australian satellites; in *Experimentations* more than 30 interactive experiments are presented to visitors of all ages to operate themselves.

Above: Harris Street entrance to the Powerhouse Museum

Below: Early steam locomotive from the Museum's collection

Other collections of decorative arts include metals, textiles, jewellery, furniture, fans, costumes, ceramics and glassware; there are pocket sundials, horse-drawn buses, early telephones, radios, phonographs, mechanical television sets and a 1,600 piece miniature car collection gathered together over 41 years. There is also a cinema: *King's*, recreated in the Art Deco style and giving visitors the chance to see silent films and news clips.

The museum possesses a wealth of information on the popular aspects of the country's history. Everything — from old pub signs, to the canvas and wood Bleriot XI Monoplane flown by French aviator Maurice Guillaux on the first airmail flight from Melbourne to Sydney in 1914 — has been compiled to create a panorama of 200 years of modern Australian social history.

The hundred-year-old complex working model of a Strasbourg clock, part of the 'Recollections' exhibition in the Museum

Central Railway Station

The Sydney area has just under 600 suburbs and 500 kilometres (300 miles) of electrified railway track, including an underground system. Electric trains run as far as Lithgow and Gosford. A large number of suburban and country commuters travel to and from the city each day. All railroads into Sydney converge at the massive Central Railway Station at the southern end of George Street.

Built in the ornate *Queen Anne* style, the station was opened in 1906, as a stirring marvel of twentieth century technology. Situated on Railway Square, the then-centre of the city, it not only linked Sydney with the rest of the country, but also used reinforced concrete (concrete with wires running through it) for the first time in an Australian building.

The University of Sydney (Australia's Oldest University)

Sydney's beginnings coincided with a period in world architecture when the designers of buildings looked to the distant past for inspiration. Consequently Sydney's nineteenth century structures look old enough to have been in place for more than six hundred years, even though they were erected in an era when trains were already trying to run on time.

The central block of the University of Sydney is one of the more graceful creations of the period which bequeathed so much 'instant tradition' on the city. The buildings rise on the hills of Camperdown, past Central Railway Station at the end of Broadway, and form the core of the oldest of Australia's tertiary institutions.

The complex of towers, archways, gargoyles-capped galleries was built in 1854, in a mixture of *Early English Gothic* and *Tudor* styles — architect Edmund Blacket considering them his finest work. The edifice, unchanged today, comprises halls and lecture rooms, fine stained-glass windows, offices for the senior professors, and a museum.

The principal facade of the building overlooks the city and is 125 metres (406 feet) long. It has a clock-tower with a carillon and encloses a quadrangle modelled on those of the ancient English colleges. Here students and visitors lounge, debate, sleep, or study on the baize-green lawns.

The best-known part of the complex is the Great Hall, where graduations and special ceremonies take place. The Hall is 41 metres (133 feet) long, 14 metres (45½ feet) wide and 23 metres (75 feet) high, its interior elaborately finished, with an open-timber roof faced with Australian cedar. Rows of stained-glass windows celebrate British royalty and the real and presumed founders of English universities.

At the southern end of the main quadrangle is the Nicholson Museum, housing the best collection of antiquities in Australia. Exhibits cover world history from the earliest times, perhaps the loveliest among them being the statue of Hermes, messenger of

Left: The University Clock Tower overlooking the City

The Quadrangle, with Nicholson Museum entrance to the left

the gods — an early Roman copy of Praxiteles' 4th century B.C. Greek original.

Opposite the gothic complex stands the modern and handsome University Library. Completed in the 1960s it contains over two million books — its rare books collection (including some printed before 1600) numbers well over 40,000; one of the rarest is Isaac Newton's *Principia Mathematica*, with the scientist's own annotations for the second edition.

The rest of the university sprawls over an enormous area, spanning three suburbs and encompassing a great variety of departments, lecture halls, colleges of various religious denominations, more museums, sports fields, meeting halls, offices, theatres and research facilities.

Interior of the 130-year-old Great Hall, scene of tens of thousands of graduation ceremonies

El Alamein Fountain at
Kings Cross

Placed at the intersection of Darlinghurst Road and Macleay
Street in a pleasant park of palms, ferns and Moreton Bay fig
trees, the fountain is poised at the heart of Kings Cross — one
of Sydney's most dynamic inner-city areas. A region of hotels,
both elegant and modest, the Cross has numerous restaurants
(ranging from French, German, Italian, and Greek, to Japanese,
Korean, Chinese, Vietnamese and Thai) most of them open late
into the night.

This ephemeral fountain was erected in 1961, around the time
that Yuri Gagarin was first orbiting the Earth in 'Sputnik'.
Designed by Robert R. Woodward and Phill Taranto, the work is
a 'sculpture in water', reflecting both the sun and the lights of
Kings Cross. Crowning a multi-tiered pool, it commemorates
the decisive North African battle of El Alamein where Australian
troops were killed in 1942.

Light and approachable, the fountain using water as its
sculptural material rather than metal or stone, was at the time an
artistic breakthrough not only in Australia, but the rest of the
world, A bronze core spouts water in the shape of a perfect
sphere through 211 nozzles, at the rate of 1,575 litres (346
gallons) per minute. Copied later in Europe, America and Asia,
the Fountain is one of Sydney's most photographed landmarks.

Elizabeth Bay House

This elegant colonial mansion was built by John Verge — a descendant of generations of Hampshire stonemasons. He came to Australia from England at the age of 42 to create a series of Regency-style buildings for a colonial aristocracy whose principal aim was to impress while advancing themselves on convict slave labour.

The house was completed for the all-powerful Colonial Secretary of the times — Alexander Macleay — in the 1830s. Described by contemporaries as the finest home in the colony, the building is now a museum in a harbourside setting.

The museum's rooms have been faithfully restored in the period of 1835-50, presenting an evocative impression of nineteenth century life with furnishings and artworks of the late Regency and early-Victorian eras. The house's most striking and renowned feature is the elliptical salon with its sweeping geometric staircase.

Situated below Kings Cross, Elizabeth Bay is an area of old mansions and modern apartment buildings. It was once the residence of Sydney's aristocracy. Later it became home to Sydney's bohemia. Since the Second World War it has been populated by a varied racial mixture.

Elizabeth Bay House — a museum of early colonial life

47 | Old Darlinghurst Prison

Situated off Taylor Square, behind the Criminal Court, the old Darlinghurst Prison is as grusome as ever. Though it houses the National Art School — and the round Cell Block at the centre of the complex has been transformed into a hall for the performing arts — the grim spell of the buildings has not been diminished over the years.

The 7-metre-high (23 feet) sandstone walls, built in the 1820s, enclose an area of about 2.2 hectares (5½ acres). Sentries were stationed on the walls, wide enough for parades to be staged on them. The quarters the convicts occupied consisted of a series of wings radiating from a central tower — over a thousand souls were imprisoned at any one time.

The discipline was suitably harsh. The high slit windows along Forbes street gave onto the flogging rooms inside — which in their time saw more than one million lashes administered to the prisoners. Not long ago a medical researcher broke off a piece of sandstone from the flooring and, through careful analysis, obtained a positive blood count — that much blood had been saturated into the stones over the years.

Inside the old gaol: the chapel is to the right. Condemned men were executed in a Y-shaped courtyard, past the chimney in the background and near the Burton Street wall

The Criminal Court

The Classic and Gothic schools of architecture were largely imposed upon nineteenth century Sydney by Mortimer Lewis, the Colonial Architect of the 1840s. Lewis was schizophrenic when it came to architecture and worked, without any conflict, in two contrasting styles. By designing his churches in Early English Gothic and his court houses in Classical Greek, he strongly influenced the course of Sydney architecture for the next 125 years.

The Darlinghurst Courthouse, on Taylor Square, still used as a criminal court today, was the high point of Lewis' determination to give Sydney correctly-proportioned public buildings. Its design and construction in 1842 constituted the pinnacle of Classical architecture in Australia.

Built hard up against the back of Darlinghurst Prison — to facilitate the trial and sentencing of prisoners — this Greek Doric sandstone courthouse soon became the pride of the city. Here were tried some of Sydney's most notorious criminals, many of whom later had successful careers in politics and business.

The Darlinghurst Court was connected to the Gaol behind it by a subterranean passage to prevent escapes

49 The Victoria Army Barracks

A true creation of the British Empire, this Paddington bulwark, with its complex of structures, was built by transported convicts and is surrounded by massive stone walls stretching over an area of 14 hectares (35 acres). Inside is a vast parade ground; a Regency building 227 metre (738 feet) long and said to be the longest in Australia; a Georgian style Officers' Quarters; a guardhouse put together with hand-made nails, and numbers of other annexes from the Victorian era.

All these elements combine to make the Barracks not only the largest — but also the most interesting relic of the British army's rule of Australia. Today the Barracks are the property of the Australian Commonwealth Government, and utilised by the Australian Armed Forces.

Outside the main gates on Oxford Street, near the Paddington Town Hall, stands the stone archway which has seen thousands of Australian troops march off to numerous wars in Africa, Europe and Asia over the past 100 years. Here, too, the Guards are solemnly changed at 10 am each Tuesday from mid-February to December. Following this martial ceremony, the Barracks and its comprehensive Military Museum are open to visitors.

Part of the facade of the longest building in Australia

Wonderful Old Paddington

Paddington is perhaps the best-known suburb in Sydney. Built on hilly ground, its houses (mostly white with iron-lace decorated balconies) follow like dainty dancers the contours of the meandering streets. The suburb began as a village for the people who built the Victoria Barracks in the 1840s — at a time when Aboriginals still inhabited the area's woodland. By the 1880s the Aboriginals had been killed or chased out, and Paddington had taken the form it has preserved for the past 100 years.

The Paddington Town Hall, built in a record time of 11 months, was completed in 1891 and has served as a place for glittering balls and Masonic Lodge meetings. Situated at the corner of Oxford Street and Oatley Road, it now houses a library, cinema and community centre.

Across the road in Oxford Street (once known as Old South Head Road), stands the lovely Juniper Hall dating from 1824, and now a children's museum with over 2,000 toys, books, prints and various exhibitions.

Paddington Town Hall along Oxford Street

51 | Centennial Park

In 1824, Governor Bourke directed the convicts of the colony to dig a 3.6 kilometre (2.2 mile) tunnel from the swamps outside Sydney, to Hyde Park, with the intention of bringing fresh water into the city. Working with bare hands for 10 years, the convicts removed 85,000 cubic metres (900,000 cubic feet) of soil, and created a conduit 2 metres wide and 1.5 metre high — large enough to supply fresh water to 20,000 people.

When an alternative water supply was found some years later, the swamps at the edge of Paddington were drained and the beautified grounds turned into parkland. Completed for the anniversary of the founding of Sydney in 1888 the grounds were named Centennial Park, and comprised paperbark fringed lakes, lawns, paths, statues, animal sanctuaries and an ambience echoing the parks of faraway Victorian England.

A century later, Centennial Park retains its nineteenth century atmosphere. Its five monumental gateways lock into 8 kilometres (4.8 miles) of 2.5 metre (8 feet) high iron fencing set in solid stone bases. Internal roads connect all parts of the park. Tame cockatoos, swans and ibis cohabit with motorists, cyclists, horses-for-hire, picnickers, kite-fliers, joggers and city dogs delirious at being unleashed to frolic.

View of English-style landscapes in Centennial Park

Above: Cockatoos and ibis on the shores of the park's ponds

Left: Black swan preening. Until the discovery of Australia's West Coast black swans were unknown in the world

Below: The commemorative bi-centennial Federation Pavilion

One of the most central golf courses in the world, in an area known in the nineteenth century as Billygoat Swamp

52 Moore Park Golf Course

Situated in historic Moore Park, a mere 4 kilometres (2.5 miles) from the city centre — between Centennial Park and South Dowling Street — this circuit is the most centrally-located championship golf course in any city in the world. The 5,887 metre (6,377 yards), 70-par layout, has tree-lined fairways, pretty American style greens and is banked with sloping hills. Open to the public, it is located at Sydney's sporting heart, within walking distance of the Cricket, Show and Sports Grounds.

Originally Moore Park was the source of Sydney's fresh water — later it became the location of a zoological garden (for 40 years) until the animals were moved to Taronga. The Park was also the site, in 1884, of the first golfing competition held in New South Wales — at the time the course had six holes. The present public course, one of 30 available in Sydney, was designed in 1911 and has one of the best records for producing champions in this country.

53 | Sparkling Bondi Beach

Beaches form an integral part of Sydney life. There are well over twenty five wonderful beaches along the city's coastline — young, old; handsome, ugly; thin and fat — all Sydneysiders sit, swim and play together in the bright democracy of the Australian sea-side.

Seashores are patrolled most of the year by members of the *Surf Life Saving Association of Australia* — founded in 1907. Lifesavers also hold beach carnivals consisting of competitions in rescue-and-resuscitation, marching, racing surf boats and swimming in enormous ocean waves.

Equally famous are the sharks around the coastline. A distinctive ringing bell is the indication of a shark alarm, upon which the native (or visitor) should discreetly depart from the water as fast as they can. Most of Sydney's surf beaches, in fact, have been meshed with anti-shark nets and the number of attacks has declined over the years.

Bondi Beach is the closest ocean beach to the city — sparkling, broad and long, it is 8 kilometres (5 miles) away, and can attract well over 25,000 people at a time. With its mixed crowds, topless bathing and general carnival atmosphere, Bondi is the best-known beach in Australia. It faces south east, but it is sheltered from strong winds: and the fine, soft, pale hour-glass sand is a pleasure to lie upon.

Bondi Beach, with the rocks of Ben Buckler at the far end

Vaucluse House

Began in 1803, this building was acquired by William Charles Wentworth in 1827. Wentworth, the 'father of the Australian Constitution' made the place his home between 1827-1853. His lavish renovations commenced in 1830 and the result is a utopian version of an English country seat — interesting for its historic associations and the elegance of its interiors.

The house is in the fashionable Early English Gothic style of the 1830s, with turrets and castellations, and visitors cannot fail to be affected by this stately, well-sited reminder of a gentry seeking the past — with floor tiles imported from Pompeii, and furniture from the Doge's Palace in Venice.

There are 15 rooms, furnished in the period of the mid-nineteenth century, and including a suite of elegant entertainment rooms, bedrooms, and a kitchen wing. Adjoining stables incorporate the grooms' quarters and hay loft, a laundry and other out-buildings.

In 1910 the house passed from Wentworth's descendants to become a State museum with colourful exhibits on colonial domestic life. There is a fine garden with parkland covering 11 hectares (27 acres) and its own harbourside beach. Devonshire teas and light meals are served and the coquettish gardens full of flowers are ideal for visits and picnics.

When the building was began, Vaucluse was still an island

The Gap — Suicide Spot of Sydney

From the city's beginnings, Sydney's population has known the meaning of despair. Brought here by the tens-of-thousands, British convicts lived in poverty, hunger and isolation. Alcoholism, crime and misery walked hand in hand. The humiliation suffered seemed to have no end — death and suicide were on the minds of many. (The number of those who *did* kill themselves, however, is not known, since attempted suicide was for years a punishable crime in Australia.) But *kill* themselves many did — either by the knife or gun, by the bottle — or by hurling themselves off The Gap.

Over the past 100 years the Gap has acquired fame as the favourite spot of those who wished to die. Romantic and grizzly, the place is on a high cliff overlooking the Pacific Ocean, a short distance from the harbour mouth. After a brief climb from Old South Head Road in Watson's Bay, the visitor reaches Gap Park and the tremendous view over the ocean and the coastline — a sight both mighty and overpowering. The ocean seems to stretch to infinity, the rocky earth seems lonely and forgotten. One can obtain a realisation of just how far Australia is from the rest of the world — and of how isolated it indeed was, for the first 150 years of its modern settlement.

The Gap — popular with Japanese honeymooning couples

56 The Fascinating Harbour Islands

Sailing into Sydney in 1788, the British were stunned with the vastness of the harbour before them. They were equally impressed with the harbour's 13 islands, and soon put most of them to use.

First of these was *Bennelong Island*. After arrival, the fleet's animals were put ashore on a small island to the east of today's Circular Quay. When Phillip, the first Governor, later ordered the capture of an Aboriginal for the purpose of studying and befriending him, a brick hut was built on the island to house the captive, whose name was Bennelong.

A few years later, while Bennelong was being taken as an exhibit on a journey to England and being introduced in London to King George III, the narrow channel between the tiny island and the town was filled in by back-breaking convict labour and given the name of Bennelong Point. Today the place is none other than the site of the Sydney Opera House.

Berry Island, by contrast, has preserved much of its unique rugged bushland. A large rock on the island's western side features an ancient 10 metre (32½ feet) Aboriginal carving of a sea monster. (A tradition is that the Camaraigal tribe who inhabited the region slew the monster with a well-aimed boomerang and the creature sank into the Harbour.) Potholes used by Aboriginals to collect water, and axe-grinding grooves in the surrounding rocks, can also be viewed.

Clark Island rises 350 metres (379 yards) north of Darling Point and was known to the Aboriginals as 'Billongoola'. The island has been the site of many events in Sydney's history, and during World War Two a Japanese midget submarine which had made its way into the harbour to fire upon the suburb of Rose Bay, was captured and stored here. The island, a nature reserve since 1870, has been developed into a native garden. Along with nearby *Shark Island* (where hibiscus and coral trees have been conserved) and *Rodd Island*, in Iron Cove, where French biologist Louis Pasteur's nephew conducted his rabbit cholera experiments in 1888, is well worth a visit.

The best-known of Sydney Harbour's islands, however, is *Fort Denison*, positioned north-east of the Opera House. Offering a desolate and rugged appearance to the colonising British, the island with its 25 metre (81 feet) high rock jutting from the water, quickly became a 'prison within a prison'. Convicts in need of 'exemplary punishment' were sent there and kept chained under the open sky for a week at a time.

One particular convict — Francis Morgan, found guilty of murder — was hung in chains and left on the gibbet post on the rock's summit. When asked if he had any last words, Morgan's reputed reply was 'Well, it certainly is a fine harbour you have

Fort Denison, built to withstand a Russian invasion. In the background the buildings of McMahon's Point and North Sydney

here'. Left in place for years, his bones were the introduction that countless newly-arrived convicts had to Sydney Harbour. (The Aboriginals believed that Morgan's ghost had the power to grab passing people by the throat.)

At a later date in the nineteenth century, Fort Denison (originally named *Rock Island*) was turned into a fortress to guard the harbour against possible Russian invasions. The sombre military fort built there from the original rock, now offset by beautiful gardens, is a popular visiting spot, commanding from all angles the beautiful harbour vista.

57 Taronga Park Zoo

Occupying 32 hectares (83 acres) of wooded hillside, the Taronga Zoo on the harbour's northern shores is home to 4,000 native and exotic animals in a secluded bushland setting. Next to it, and running down to Bradley's Head, is Ashton Park — a popular public reserve.

The name Taronga is an adaptation of an Aboriginal word meaning 'beautiful water view', and the Zoo has been located on this spot since 1916, when the original animals were moved from cramped quarters at Moore Park where they had been resident since 1881. The Zoo's present site is one of the most scenic spots in Sydney.

Taronga features a Koala House, a Rainforest Aviary, a Nocturnal House (for viewing small night-time marsupials by

Zoo entrance built in the 1910s

Above: The world's favourite pet — the koala
Below: Australia's most loved animal — the wombat

simulated moonlight), a 'Platypusary' (permitting the observation of platypuses underwater), a spacious Chimpanzee Park, an Aquarium, a pool which stages regular acrobatic displays by Australian fur seals, and a Waterhole Complex (where animals can be observed drinking and resting as they might in the wild).

The ramp at *Koala House* enables the visitor to get eye-level with these amiable tree-dwelling animals by means of a wooden walkway.

The *Rainforest Aviary*, inside a giant transparent enclosure, exhibits birds from Australia and tropical New Guinea in exotic surroundings.

Friendship Farm permits children to touch domesticated animals such as lambs, goats, donkeys, chickens, and even wallabies.

The Australian and New Zealand fur seals joyously thrive in a wave tank, while their remarkable aquatic performances are held in the *Seal Theatre* twice daily.

The *Aquarium* displays 550 species of fish in 43 different types of habitat tanks simulating natural riverbed, coral reef and open sea environments. The *Platypusary* contains, in addition to the platypus, the echidna — together these two animals are the world's only *monotremes* (or egg-laying mammals).

Platypuses, *Ornithorhynchus anatinus*, though classed as marsupials, do not have marsupial-style pouches in which to grow their young. The mother lays eggs which she hatches by adopting a curled posture, with the tail laid over the egg on the underside of its body. Nor do the females have teats — the milk is transferred to the young through the skin.

During the breeding season, the female echidna, *Tachyglossus*, develops a simple pouch into which she consequently lays a single egg. This takes about 10 days to hatch and the young echidna is carried in its mother's pouch for about 3 months.

Echidnas have been known to live for 10 years in captivity

58 | The Ocean Beach at Manly

A narrow isthmus between the Pacific Ocean and the northern waters of Sydney Harbour, Manly may be reached either by road or one of the ferries which criss-cross the Harbour.

The ocean beach remains its greatest attraction. A sandy stretch lined with Norfolk Island pine trees, it faces the ocean and is usually sheltered from the cold north-east and southerly winds.

Australian surf riding had its beginnings in Manly where a young man from the New Hebrides, Tommy Tanna, introduced it to the local youths in the 1890s.

Public-bathing in the ocean likewise began here. In 1902 it was still forbidden to bathe or swim publicly in Australia between the daylight hours of 6 am and 8 pm. In that year, a Manly newspaper proprietor announced that he intended to break the law and go for a swim in the full light of day wearing a neck-to-knee costume. Thousands of onlookers gathered to watch the editor's fearless action. Through his initiative, and following an intensive campaign, the law which allowed day-time swimming was passed in 1903.

Underwaterland situated on Manly harbour, is Australia's first oceanarium. It has displays of live sharks caught in the Sydney region. (Sharks, like tigers, conjure emotive images of primitive

The Norfolk Pine trees of Manly Beach

forces beyond reach of pity or emotion; yet more people are killed on Australia's roads in a few months than have been taken by sharks in the whole of the country's recorded history; estimates of the total number of shark-attack victims in the past 200 years vary from 100 to 450.)

Adjacent to Underwaterland at the far end of the West Esplanade, the Manly Art Gallery, offers a fine selection of paintings, and temporary exhibitions on varied subjects ranging from surfing to nude bathing.

The Corso, Manly's main thoroughfare, is a plaza safe from motor traffic; full of shops, cafes and restaurants, it leads from the ferry wharf to the ocean front. There is a pleasant pathway past the surf club at the beach's southern end, along Fairy Bower and on to Shelley Beach and another section of the reserve which covers North Head.

Placed on the cliff-tops at Manly is St Patrick's College — Australia's oldest and one time only Roman Catholic theological seminary. It has a fine collection of some 60,000 theological books drawn from the various monastic libraries of Europe.

Landmark on the hill on the east of Manly — St Patrick's College

Splendours of Barrenjoey Head

When the British exploration vessel *Endeavour* left Botany Bay on 7 May 1770 to travel northwards along the coastline, Captain James Cook found himself the afternoon of the same day sailing at a short distance from some irregular land which seemed to form an enclave. Naming the place Broken Bay, he never suspected that this was the mouth of a great river (later to be named the Hawkesbury) hidden from the sea by Barrenjoey Head.

Barrenjoey is on a peninsula 41 kilometres (24.6 miles) north of the city and offers some of the most exhilarating vistas of Sydney's coastline. At its, after a climb of 110 metres (357 feet), the visitor discovers the 16 metre (52 feet) high Barrenjoey light-house. Built in 1880, it is one of the most powerful in the country. The grave of the first light-house keeper is nearby — he died when struck by a bolt of lightning.

A bounty of 24 magnificent beaches can be discovered on a stretch of 25 kilometres (15 miles) along the Manly-Warringah peninsula, from the North Head in Sydney Harbour to the tip of Barrenjoey Head. The visitor will appreciate sensations of vastness and freedom, and experience the spirit of Australia's seaside.

View from Barrenjoey Head looking towards Barrenjoey and Palm Beach; Ku-ring-gai Chase National Park is on the right

60 La Perouse

In January 1788 one of the most remarkable encounters in history took place on the edge of the then-known world. Two French ships, *L'astrolabe* and *La boussole* — under command of the Count of La Perouse — sailed into Botany Bay to encounter part of the British Admiralty's fleet laden with convicts ready to colonise the newly discovered continent.

Having sailed from France in August 1785, the Count of La Perouse had made extensive explorations of the North Pacific. The ships then made for Botany Bay as the French had heard in China that a British settlement was being formed there.

At the bay, the French built a stockade, buried a Franciscan monk whose tomb can still be seen today, were visited by British officers thirsty for champagne and by convicts trying to escape. La Perouse then sailed from the bay on 10 March — and nothing more was ever heard of him or his ships.

The La Perouse Museum commemorates this expedition and the unsolved mystery that still surrounds the fate of its members. Housed in the restored Cable Station of 1882, on the shores of Frenchmen's Bay, the exhibition consists of original charts and maps, navigational instruments, portraits and depictions of the peoples encountered on the voyage.

Nearby, at the tip of the peninsula and joined to the mainland by a bridge, is Bare Island. Dramatically situated at the entrance to Botany Bay, the island houses a nineteenth century fort which once constituted part of Sydney's defences, Events surrounding the history of the fort are depicted in a museum inside the barracks.

Further to the east, set right on the Pacific Ocean, are two rugged and spectacular golf courses. The grandeur of their rocky coastline is most reminiscent of the famous St Andrews course in Scotland. The New South Wales Club course is 6,232 metres (6,751 yards) long. Golfers hit their tee shots across foaming surf and are subject to every whim of the ocean breezes. Adjoining on a salty windswept headland, is St Michaels, with a 5,854 metres (6,342 yards) long course, — per 72. It features fairways across deep ravines, and greens fiercely guarded on both sides by thick scrub and sand dunes.

Bare Island at the entrance to Botany Bay. The disused fort, now a museum, is linked to the mainland by a bridge. It was christened 'Bare' by Captain Cook in 1770

The La Perouse Museum, housed in the old Cable Station which once linked Australia telegraphically with the rest of the world. In the foreground, the monument raised by the French to the memory of La Perouse. To the right, the Macquarie Watchtower, (built c. 1820) and used against smugglers

61 Australia's Birthplace

By the middle of the eighteenth century European navigators had charted a large part of the globe. The Antipodes, however, still remained a mystery — the enigma of the 'Great South Land', a continent suspected to exist on the basis of a map published in Dieppe in 1566. Australia, the elusive continent, seemed to keep evading discovery. At times, the more daring explorers stumbled onto promontories, long barren coastlines and inhospitable cliffs scattered over an enormous area stretching from the Indian Ocean well into the Pacific — but not one among them dared to suppose that all these separate entities fitted into one enormous landmass.

Then, on 19 April 1770, the officer on watch aboard the *Endeavour* — a British vessel commanded by Captain James Cook — sighted the eastern shore of Australia. In a momentous discovery, the Great South Land the Captain had been seeking had at last been found. Cook promptly steered his course northward and some time later stumbled onto Botany Bay — a spacious harbour which today is part of southern Sydney. Here he stepped ashore and skirmished with the local Aboriginals on behalf of his master the British King George III.

Traditionally, Cook's landing site at Kurnell on Botany Bay is seen as the true birthplace of modern Australia. Discovered at 3 pm on 29 April 1770, and first visited by a white during Cook's week-long stay there, the area has more or less been left as the Captain found it. Two centuries later, this landing place south of the city at the extreme tip of the Kurnell Peninsula is a public reserve marked with monuments and a museum devoted to the life and travels of Captain James Cook.

Approaching the landing place by the path running around the point at the waterline, the visitor first comes to Captain Cook's Well. According to tradition, this is one of the pits sunk by the crew to get fresh water. Next, on some rocks a few metres from the shoreline's high-tide, is the spot where Isaac Smith set foot as the first white man in New South Wales. Further along, opposite the spot where the *Endeavour*'s crew landed, Cook's Obelisk rises — erected in 1870.

Similarly there are memorials raised to Cook's companions — the botanist Joseph Banks (he gave the bay its name) and to the naturalist Daniel Solander (a Swede) — while another tablet marks the spot where Cook oversaw the burial of Forby Sutherland, the first British subject to be buried in Australian soil.

Upon the hill, the Captain Cook Museum has displays of Cook's life, travels and discoveries, as well as artifacts from the *Endeavour*.

Monument at Kurnell erected to the memory of Captain Cook

The Royal National Park

Created in 1879, this park was the first national park in the country, and is indeed the second oldest national park in the world. It is one of great Australian reserves and offers opportunities for scenic drives, picnics, long or short bushwalks, fishing, surfing, canoeing and climbing. Its eastern boundary consists of 14 kilometres (8 miles) of Pacific sea-coast, with fine sandy beaches.

Situated 36 kilometres (21.5 miles) south of Sydney, the park is also a 15,000 hectare (40,000 acre) sanctuary for more than 700 species of flowers, 250 bird species (many of them tame) and a number of marsupials, including the echidna and swamp wallaby.

The high ground of the park is a windswept plateau with deep ravines. There are some breath-taking bushwalks along the cliff tops — Robertson's Knoll offers excellent panoramic views of Sydney. In late winter and early spring the park is carpeted with wildflowers typical to the region.

Some of the extensive pathways were made by the district's original inhabitants — Aboriginals of the Dharawal tribe. Others have been made by cattle and deer — the deer, first brought into the park in the 1880s, congregate before sunset in the areas near Garie and Era beaches.

In the gullies, the Hacking River (named after the quartermaster of the First Fleet of 1788) and its tributaries run the full length of the region. Visitors can hire rowboats at the village of Audley for the opportunity of viewing swans, wild ducks and tame lyre-birds (which are plentiful) — and it is by water that the most extravagant and interesting landscapes in the park may be seen.

Beautiful Wattamola Beach on the Pacific Ocean coast

*Top: The Azure Kookaburra, a patient hunter;
Bottom: Banksia*

⟨63⟩ Historic Sites of Parramatta

Parramatta is the second oldest centre of civilised settlement in Australia. It lies 25 kilometres (15 m) west of the City and forms the geographical centre of the greater Sydney region.

It was founded by Governor Phillip in 1788 when the agricultural land that was available in Sydney proved of very poor quality. Travelling up Sydney Harbour, the Governor came upon the fertile shores of the Parra River (in Aboriginal Parramatta meant 'head of the river'), and founded there a new settlement which soon prospered.

The classically elegant Old Government House stands in Parramatta Park on the site of a tiny cottage built in 1790 for Governor Phillip. Though of military simplicity, the spacious and airy building has a classical portico and fanlight, and lovely Australian cedar fireplaces. With a pleasant outlook over the gardens, it soon became the favourite residence of the early Governors.

The house, property of the National Trust of Australia, has been restored and furnished in period style. Of particular interest are Governor Macquarie's bedroom, dressing room and breakfast room, along with pieces of Australian colonial furniture original to the building.

Parramatta has many other places of interest, among them the impressive modern Sports Stadium; King's — Australia's oldest school; St Patrick's — the site of the first Catholic mass said in Australia; Lennox Bridge — built across the river in 1836 and oldest of all the Sydney Harbour bridges.

There are also the historic buildings of Brislington, Harrisford House and Hambledon Cottage; the Lancer Army Barracks — Australia's oldest army barracks built in 1820; Experiment Farm Cottage — originating from 1793; Elizabeth Farm — Australia's oldest building (See following story); and St John's Church on the corner of Macquarie and Church streets.

Experiment Farm Cottage, built in 1793, belonged to James Ruse — the first European to set foot on Sydney Cove. The building and its grounds are maintained as a museum dedicated to the colony's history and early farming days. The farm produced the first commercially sold wheat harvest in Australia.

The Anglican church of St John's began life in 1788 as a hut with open air services conducted by the Chaplain of the First Fleet. The chapel grew to become the first official church in the Colony. The distinctive pair of brick towers with pyramidal rooftops were added in 1820 at the suggestion of Mrs Macquarie, the Governor's wife.

*Old Government House in Parramatta Park, erected in 1799. A
favourite spring residence of the early governors, now a museum*

St John's — one of the oldest churches in Australia

Elizabeth Farm

The picturesque Elizabeth Farm is at Sydney's western limit — in Parramatta, Australia's second oldest settlement, and today a part of the city.

The farm serves as a museum of colonial life. Commenced in 1793 — the year French King Louis XVI was beheaded — the building is the oldest in Australia, and intricately linked with the country's history and agricultural development. It was to Elizabeth Farm that some of the first merino sheep were brought, in an experiment which was to revolutionise the economy and make the words 'Australia' and 'wool' synonymous for 150 years.

Furnished in the manner of the early nineteenth century, the museum features canopied beds, polished floors and paintings of its original owners — John and Elizabeth Macarthur. In the arrangement of its rooms in a straight line, the building allows effective cross-ventilation and interior cooling by the evening breezes during high summer. Elizabeth Farm was the first farmhouse of its kind, and the prototype of later farmhouses across New South Wales.

In the 1830s the famous builder John Verge extended and altered the house, which acquired joinery in elegantly-worked cedar, and a 'hipped' roof — the distinctive silhouette still associated with Australian farmhouses today.

Wildlife Parks of Sydney

What Renaissance art is to Italy — marsupials are to Australia. Overseas Visitors often make a 10,000 kilo-metre journey with the chief aim of clasping a koala to their breasts. While tourists travel to Florence to stand before Botticelli's *Venus*, they travel to Sydney to cuddle a koala.

Within an hour's drive from the City are several wildlife sanctuaries where the marsupials and birds of Australia may be inspected at close range. Koalas, kangaroos, wombats, dingos, possums, Tasmanian devils, echidnas, emus, cockatoos, kooka-burras, and visitors — are all free to roam about and observe each other at leisure.

Waratah Park, in Duffys Forest, overlooks the Hawkesbury River and has been devised to resemble the backlot of an animal film studio. Visitors can meet kangaroos and koalas dressed up as movie stars, and travel on a scenic bush railway on an inspection tour of the grounds.

Young kangaroo, known as a 'joey'

Featherdale Wildlife Park, in Doonside near Blacktown, allows the visitor to pat and feed animals in a natural environment. Peacocks, lyre birds, lorikeets and other Australian avians are also on display. In a special enclosure wombats (though a protected species) are permitted to play with visiting children.

Koala Park, in Pennant Hills, was Sydney's first koala sanctuary — founded in the 1930s. It allows the animals to roam in total freedom, with the chance of having their photographs taken with the visitors. The park is also home to hundreds of native plants, some of which live for a 1,000 years.

There are about 45 different species of kangaroos and wallabies in Australia. (The scientific name for the species is *macropod* or 'big foot'.) The pouch under the female kangaroo's stomach is called a *marsupium*. The newborn baby is small — about the size of a thumb-nail. After birth, it climbs through the mother's fur to her pouch. Here it remains for the next six months. and is called a joey.

Kangaroos and wallabies are grazing animals, living on herbage and plants. The largest species grow to a height of over 2 metres (6.5 feet). The tree kangaroo can make jumps of 9 metres (29 feet). Like the rat, the red kangaroo keeps growing all its life.

In the nineteenth century, Australia was famous for her kangaroos. In the twentieth century, however, the *koala* has become the indisputable star of the continent.

Koalas have soft ash-coloured fur, a docile 'teddy bear' expression, a paw with 2 thumbs and 3 fingers, and a diet consisting of eucalyptus leaves. The females have a pouch opening towards the rear, and powerful abdominal muscles to hold their babies in securely.

Like other marsupials, the newborn koala is woefully undeveloped; it is the size of a glacé cherry. Unaided, it drags itself into the mother's pouch to stay there attached to a teat. After seven months it emerges to ride on the mother's back, or rests cuddled against her chest while she sleeps. At one year of age it starts life on its own. In their natural state koalas seldom drink (the name is Aboriginal for 'no water'); they prefer solitude, and it is more common to see a single animal than a colony. The average life span is 10-20 years. Males that cannot find a partner to mate with often stop eating and pine away.

While koalas are loved by tourists and visitors, the animal closest to the heart of *Australians* is the wombat. This creature is built like a small army tank; stout and sturdy, it is possessed with the determination to go wherever it desires to by the most direct route.

Big-headed and small-eyed, the animal grows to about 1.3 metres in length and can weigh 36 kilograms. It eats roots, shoots and leaves, and digs its way into underground burrows up to 30 metres (97 feet) deep. In captivity wombats have been known to live up to 27 years.

The newborn wombat is less than 3 centimetres long and weighs 1 gram when it crawls into the mother's pouch, which faces backwards to prevent dirt and twigs getting caught in it when the mother digs or climbs. The baby does not leave the pouch's safety until 7-10 months later.

Wombats have been known to make wonderful pets. A family in New South Wales kept a tame wombat which met the children outside school each day, and walked home with them like a dog. In Queensland, a wombat once trekked 20 kilometres to warn its owners that one of their family members was in danger.

Koalas live on an exclusive diet of eucalyptus leaves

66 The Blue Mountains

A unique range just 65 kilometres (39 miles) inland from Sydney, the Blue Mountains have been the city's favourite resort since the last century. Deep canyons — several kilometres wide, others merely narrow ravines — zigzag in a maze between enormous sandstone walls. Millions of years of erosion have carved sheer cliff faces and precipitous waterfalls.

Woodland, rainforest, grassland, heath and swamp are all still present, with a wide variety of gigantic eucalyptus trees and cool-climate flora, distributed over an area of 100,865 hectares (262,000 acres). The mountains are famous for their crisp, bracing air, mineral spas and walkways constructed at the turn of the century.

Kangaroos, wallabies, possums and wombats have their home here, and the trees and ferns nest thornbills, honeyeaters and thrushes. The characteristic haze given off by the evaporating oil of the eucalyptus tree forests has given the 'Blue' Mountains their name.

Perched on the edge of the Jamieson Valley, Katoomba overlooks, from Echo Point a most photogenic and identifiable rock formation called the Three Sisters; Aboriginal legends place the three mighty cliffs at the centre of a tremendous struggle between two warring tribes. Their names are Gunnedoo, Wimlah and Meenhi.

View of the 'Three Sisters' from Echo Point in Katoomba

67 Katoomba and Leura

Sydney's resorts at the top of the Blue Mountains were highly fashionable in the nineteenth century, when the colonial governors used them as their summer residence. Katoomba, 1017 metres above sea-level, was the meeting place of the well-to-do, and of numerous artists. Charles Darwin and Sarah Bernhardt both visited the place and recorded their delight at its sights.

Leura features a newly completed modern hotel, also the Everglades Garden Festival and many other famous English-style gardens. Katoomba has the unique Scenic Railway — built in the 1880s, this descends 310 metres (1007 feet) into a tree-covered gorge at an incline of 45 degrees, and is one of the steepest railways in the world.

The mountains also display their natural wonders from a horizontal cable-car, the Scenic Skyway, which runs 275 metres (900 feet) above the valley floor and offers views of Katoomba Falls, Orphan Rock and the spectacular Jamieson Valley.

One of the many attractive gardens of Leura

The Jenolan Caves

Some distance south-west of Katoomba, this extravagant series of underground limestone grottoes was discovered in the 1830s when a highwayman's victim tracked the robber down to his secret mountain hide-out.

The cave's gateway is a 24 metre (78 foot) grand arch called the Devil's Coach-house. Parts of the cave system — the longest in the world — have still not been explored, but nine impressive halls are open for inspection and more than 200,000 visitors pass through them each year.

With names like The Cathedral, The Bath of Venus, Arabesque, and Skeleton, the individual caves have natural formations with graphic titles such as The Pillar of Hercules, Angel's Wing and The Whale's Throat. (Skeleton Cave gets its name from the ancient bones of an Aboriginal embedded in the floor.)

A road from the caves leads into the 68,000 hectare (177,000 acre) Kanangra Boyd National Park, with its glorious waterfalls near the Kanangra Gorge.

The 'Devil's Coach House', near the entrance to the Caves

General Information

Anzac War Memorial: Hyde Park South, City; Tel: 267-7668; Open: Mon-Sat 10.00-16.00, Sun 13.00-16.00; Train: Museum; Bus: 111, 308-10, 373-4, 389, 396-8, 777

Art Gallery of New South Wales: Art Gallery Road, Domain; Tel 225-1700; Opening hours Mon-Sat 10-5, Sun 12-5; Train: St James or Martin Place; Bus: 111, 311, 666, 777

Australian Museum: 6-8 College Street, City; Tel: 267-7668; Open: Tue-Sun 10.00-17.00, Mon 12.00-17.00; Train: Museum; Bus: 111, 324-5, 369, 389, 399, 777

Bare Island Museum: Anzac Parade, La Perouse; Tel: 661-2397; Open: Mon-Sun 9.00-15.30; Bus: 393-4

Bondi Beach: Campbell Parade, Bondi; Bus: 365, 380, 382, 389

Blue Mountains, (Katoomba, Leura, Jenolan Caves): Information Centre, Echo Point, Katoomba; Tel: (047) 821-833; Train: Central; Bus: Private coaches

Cadman's Cottage: 110 George Street, City; Tel: 27-8861; Open: Mon-Fri 9.00-16.00; Tours: Mon-Sun 10.00-15.00 Tel 27-6678; Train: Circular Quay; Bus: 111, 324, 431, 433, 777

Captain Cook's Landing Place: Polo Street, Kurnell; Tel: 668-9923 or 668-9548; Open: Mon-Sun 7.00-19.00; Train: Cronulla, and then Bus: 67 (Sat till 12.00, not Sun)

Centennial Park: Oxford Street, Paddington; Open: Sunrise-Sunset; Bus: 339, 341, 372-4, 378, 380, 396

Central Railway Station: Railway Square, City; Tel: 20942; Train: All trains; Bus: 308-10; 341, 372, 393, 422-6, 480-3

Chinese Gardens: Darling Harbour Square, City; Open: Daily; Train: Town Hall, Monorail; Bus: 111, 429-33, 468-70, 502

Conservatorium of Music: Macquarie Street, City; Tel: 230-1222; Open: Mon-Fri 9.00-17.00; Train: Circular Quay, Martin Place; Bus: 111, 207-8, 263, 337, 399, 777

Cook Discovery Centre Museum: Polo Street, Kurnell; Tel: 668-9923 or 668-9548; Open: Mon-Sun 10.30-16.30; Train: Cronulla, and then Bus: 67 (Sat till 12.00, not Sun)

Darling Harbour Square: Darling Harbour, City; Tel: 211-2311: Train: Town Hall, Central, Monorail; Bus: 111, 429-33, 468-70, 502

Darlinghurst Court House: Taylor Square, Darlinghurst; Tel: 33-0976; Open: Mon-Fri 10.00-16.00

Darlinghurst Prison: Forbes Streets, Darlinghurst; Tel: 339-8666; Open: Mon-Fri 9.00-17.00; Bus 302-4, 311, 380, 389

Elizabeth Bay House Museum; 7 Onslow Avenue, Elizabeth Bay; Tel: 358-2344; Open: Tue-Sun 10.00-16.30; Train: Kings Cross; Bus: 111, 311

Elizabeth Farm: 70 Alice Street, Parramatta; Tel: 635-9488; Open: Tue-Sun 10.00-16.30; Train: Parramatta; Bus: Explorer

Entertainment Centre: Harbour Street, Haymarket; Tel: 211-2222; Train & Bus: See Darling Harbour

Experiment Farm Cottage: 9 Ruse Street, Parramatta; Tel: 635 5655; Open: Tue-Thu and Sun 10.00-16.00; Train: Parramatta

Featherdale Wildlife Park: 217 Kildare Road, Doonside; Tel: 622-1705; Open: Mon-Sun 9.00-17.00; Train: Emu Plains

Fort Denison: Sydney Harbour: Maritime Services Board; Tel: 27-6606; Tours: Tue-Sun 10.00, 12.30, 14.00; Ferry: No 6 Jetty, Circular Quay

Gap: Old South Head Road, Watsons Bay: Bus: 324-5, 327, Private coach tours

Garrison Church: 50 Lower Fort Street, The Rocks; Tel: 27-2664; Open: Mon-Sun 8.00-18.00; Bus: 111, 431, 433

Great Synagogue: 187a Elizabeth Street, City; Tel: 267-2477; Tours: (Entry from 166 Castlereagh Street) Tue 12.00, Thu 13.00; Train: Museum; Bus: 111, 777

Harbour Islands: Sydney Harbour National Park; Tel: 337-5511 for enquiries and tours.

Harbour Bridge Pylon Lookout: Dawes Point, Rocks; Tel: 218-6888; Open: Fri-Sun 10.00-17.00; Train: Circular Quay; Bus: 111, 431, 433

Hyde Park Museum: Queen's Square, City; Tel: 217-0333; Open: Wed-Mon 10.00-17.00, Tue 12.00-17.00; Train: St James

Juniper Hall Museum: 1 Ormond Street, Paddington; Tel 332-1988; Open: Sun 10.00-16.00; Bus: 380, 389

Koala Park Sanctuary: 84 Castle Hill Road, West Pennant Hills; Tel 484-3141; Open: 9.00-17.00; Transport Enquiries: 450-1236 or 450-2377

La Perouse Museum: Anzac Parade, La Perouse; Tel: 661-2765; Open: Mon-Fri 9.00-16.00; Bus: 393-4

Manly: Ocean Beach Road, Manly; Manly Tourist Promotions Tel: 977-1088; Ferry: No 3 Jetty, Circular Quay; Bus: 131-2, 135, 141-2

Mint Museum: Queen's Square; Tel: 217-0111; Open: Thu-Tue 10.00-17.00, Wed 12.00-17.00; Train: St James, Martin Place

Moore Park Golf: Cleveland Street and Anzac Parade, Moore Park; Tel: 663-3791; Open: Mon-Sun; Bus: 18, 303, 337, 393-4

Mrs Macquarie's Chair; Mrs Macquarie's Road, Mrs Macquarie's Point; Bus: 311, 666, 777

National Maritime Museum: Darling Harbour, City; Tel: 27-9111; Open: Mon-Sun 10.00-17.00; Train: Town Hall, Central, Monorail

Nicholson Museum; Off Main Quadrangle, University of Sydney; Parramatta Road, Camperdown; Tel: 692-2812; Open: Mon-Fri 9.00-16.00; Bus: 422-426, 435-440

Observatory Museum: Watson Road, Observatory Hill, The Rocks; Tel: 241-2478; Open: Mon-Fri 14.00-17.00 and 20.00-2.00; Bus: 111, 431

Old Government House: Parramatta Park, Parramatta; Tel: 635-8149; Open: Tue-Thu and Sun 10.00-16.00; Train: Parramatta; Bus: Explorer

Opera House; Bennelong Point, City; Tel: 250-7111; Tours: Mon-Sun 9.00-16.00; Outdoor entertainment: Sun 12.00-17.00; Train: Circular Quay; Bus: 111; Ferry: Circular Quay

Powerhouse Museum: Harris and Macarthur Streets, Ultimo; Tel: 217-0111; Open: Mon-Sun 10.00-17.00; Train: Town Hall, Central, Monorail; Bus: 422-6, 448, 460, 480-3, 502

Queen Victoria Building; George and Market Street, City; Tel: 29-1172; Open: 24 Hours; Train: Town Hall, Monorail; Bus: 111, 301-2, 429-33, 441, 460-1, 468-70, 500, 666, 777

Rocks Visitors Centre: 104 George Street, The Rocks; Tel: 27-4972; Open: Mon-Fri 8.30-16.30; Sat-Sun 10.00-17.00

Royal Botanic Gardens: Macquarie Street, City; Open: 8.00 to Sunset; Free tours: Wed-Fri 10.00, Sun 13.00

Royal National Park: The park has 60 kilometres (36 miles) of roads, mostly sealed. Visitors can drive in from the Princes Highway, or reach the park by train. A ferry service from Cronulla can take visitors to the village of Bundeena, in the north-east of the park. For boat hire Tel: 521-5633

St Andrews Cathedral; Town Hall Square, City; Tel: 265-1555; Open: Mon-Fri 7.30-18.00, Sat 9.00-16.00, Sun 8.00-20.15; Train: Town Hall; Bus: 301-2, 429-33, 460-1, 468-70, 500.

St James Church: King S   City; Tel: 232-3592; Open: Mon-Fri 8.00-18.00, Sat 8.00-17.00, Sun 8.00-16.00; Train: St James, Martin Place; Bus: 111, 308-11, 396-9, 777

St John's Church: Church Street, Parramatta; Open: Mon-Sun 9.00-15.00; Tours: Fri; Train: Parramatta; Bus: Explorer

St Mary's Cathedral; College Street, City; Tel: 232-3788; Open: Sun-Fri 6.30-19.30, Sat 8.00-19.30; Train: St James; Bus: 111, 311, 312, 399

State Library: Shakespeare Place, City; Tel: 230-1414; Open: Mon-Sat 9.00-21.00, Sun 14.00-18.00; Tours: Wed 11.00; Train: Martin Place, St James; Bus: 111, 311, 312, 777

State Parliament of New South Wales; Macquarie Street, City; Tel: 230-2111; Open: Mon-Fri 10.00-16.00; Tours. Mon-Fri 10.00-16.30; Train: Martin Place; Bus: 111, 777

Supreme Court; Elizabeth and King Streets, City; Open: Mon-Fri 10.00-16.00; Train: St James, Martin Place; Bus: 111, 311, 312, 399

Sydney Aquarium: Pier 26, Darling Harbour; Tel: 262-2300; Open: Mon-Sun 9.30-21.00; Train: Town Hall, Wynyard, Monorail; Bus: 111, 777

Sydney Hospital; Macquarie Street, City; Tel: 230-0111; Train: Martin Place, St James; Bus: 111, 311, 312, 399

Sydney Maritime Museum: Birkenhead Point, Drummoyne; Tel: 81-4374; Open: Tue-Sun 10.00-17.00, Mon 13.00-17.00; Bus: 491-4, 500-2

Sydney Town Hall: 483 George Street, City; Tel: 20263; Tours: Tue, Thu 11.00; Transport: See St Andrews Cathedral

Sydney Tower: Centrepoint, 100 Market Street, City; Tel: 229-7444; Open: Mon-Sat 9.30-21.30, Sun 10.30-18.30; Train: St James, Monorail; Bus: Most city buses

Taronga Zoo: Bradleys Head Road, Mosman; Tel: 969-2777; Open: Mon-Sun 9.00-17.00; Ferry: Circular Quay; Bus: 238

Underwaterworld: West Esplanade, Manly; Tel: 949-2644; Open: 10.00-18.00 Mon-Sun; Shows 11-16.30; Transport: See Manly

Vaucluse House: Olola Avenue, Vaucluse; Tel: 337-1957; Grounds open: 7.00-17.00; Museum open: Tue-Sun 10.00-16.30; Bus: 325, Private coach tours

Victoria Army Barracks; Oxford Street, Paddington; Tel: 399-0455; Open: Tue 10.30-12.00; Bus: 380, 389, 399

Waratah Park: Namba Road, Terrey Hills; Tel: 450-2377; Open: Mon-Sun: 10.00-17.00; Transport Tel: 450-1236 or 450-2377

Index

SYDNEY

↑
N

MILLERS
POINT

ARGYLE

THE
ROCKS
ST.

(35)

(34)

(37)

(36)

(35) (33)

(38)

CAHILL

BRIDGE

SUSSEX

KENT

CLARENCE

YORK

VINYARD
PARK

GEORGE

PITT

(30)

MARTIN

HUN

DARLING

HARBOUR

Maritime
Museum

(40)

KING

STREET

ST

MARKET

(27)

PYRMONT BRIDGE FOOTBRIDGE

Harbourside
Markets

(39)

(26)

(25)

Convention
Centre

BATHURST

STRE

LIVERPOOL

HARRIS
ST.

(42)

Exhibition
Centre

(41)

PIER

STREET

CHINATOWN

(43)

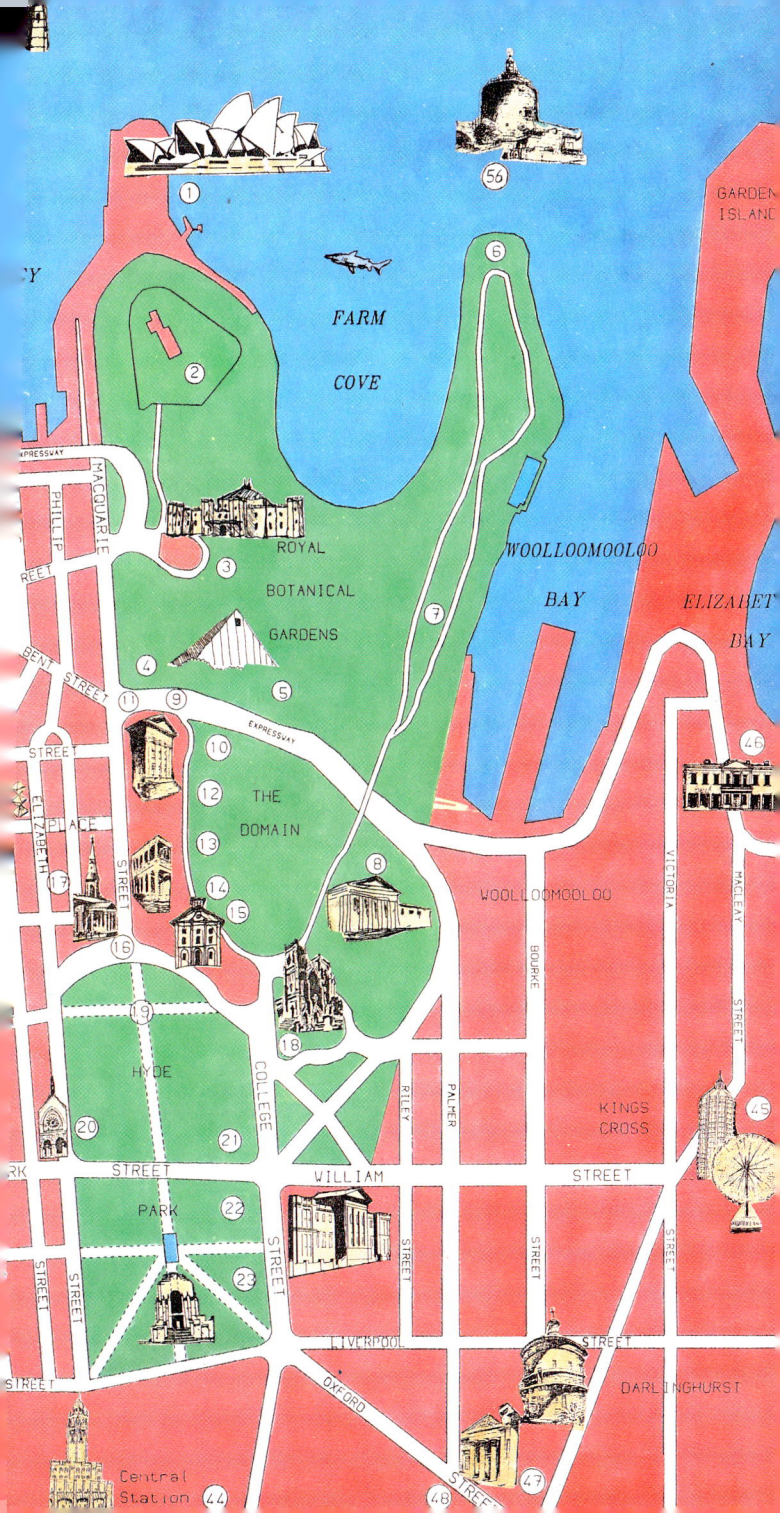

① ②

㊌ 56

GARDEN
ISLAND

FARM

COVE

⑥

WOOLLOOMOOLOO

BAY

ELIZABETH

BAY

ROYAL

BOTANICAL

GARDENS

③

④ ⑤

⑪ ⑨

⑩

⑫

THE

DOMAIN

⑬

⑭

⑮

⑧

WOOLLOOMOOLOO

⑯

⑰

⑲

HYDE

⑱

⑳

PARK

㉑

STREET

KINGS
CROSS

㊺

㉒

WILLIAM

㉓

LIVERPOOL

STREET

DARLINGHURST

OXFORD

Central
Station ㊹

STREET

㊽ ㊼

MACQUARIE

PHILLIP

BENT STREET

ELIZABETH

PLACE

ELIZABETH STREET

COLLEGE

RILEY

PALMER

BOURKE

VICTORIA

MACLEAY STREET

STREET

SYDNEY
First published 1989
Major Mitchell Press
PO Box 997, Potts Point,
2011, N.S.W., Australia

Photographs:

Lukas Roth, pages: 7, 11, 13, 14, 15, 16 (b), 17, 18, 19, 20, 25, 27, 28, 29, 31,
34, 35, 37, 42, 43, 45 (b), 47, 48, 49, 53, 55, 56, 59, 62, 63, 64, 65, 66, 68, 74, 75,
87, 90, 91, 93 (t), 94, 96, 97, 99, 103, 107, 111.

Ben Apfelbaum, pages: 6, 10, 16 (t), 33, 36, 45 (t), 57, 60, 61, 67, 70, 71, 73, 76,
77, 81, 82, 83, 85, 86, 88, 89, 92, 93 (b), 95, 100, 102, 104, 105, 109, 110, 113,
114, 115, 117, 118, 119, 120.

Additional photographs by:

Don McMurdo, pages 8, 9; Art Gallery of New South Wales: 21, 22, 23, 24; St
Mary's Cathedral: 39, 40, 41; Australian Museum: 50, Kate Lowe 51 (t), Anthony
Farr 51 (b); Powerhouse Museum: 1, 79, 80; University of Sydney: 84; Taronga
Park Zoo: 101. 111; NSW Government Printing Office: 30.

Book Design: Moi Moi
Editor: Paul Cliff
German Version: Dorte Dose
Japanese Version: Yuri Naganuma
Layout: Gianni Toncetti
Map: John O'Sullivan and Lukas Roth
Research: Lindy Sinclair

Typesetting: Keyset Phototype Sydney
Typographical Executive: Colin Lewis
Printer: Tien Wah Press Ltd, Singapore

Distribution to newsagencies by Network

National Library of Australia
Cataloguing-in-Publication Data

Treborlang, Robert
SYDNEY

ISBN 0 9587708 1 6